ADD/ADHD
ALTERNATIVES
in the classroom

THOMAS ARMSTRONG

Association for Supervision and Curriculum Development

Alexandria, Virginia USA

Association for Supervision and Curriculum Development
1703 N. Beauregard St. • Alexandria, VA 22311-1714 USA
Telephone: 1-800-933-2723 or 703-578-9600 • Fax: 703-575-5400
Web site: http://www.ascd.org • E-mail: member@ascd.org

Gene R. Carter, *Executive Director*

Michelle Terry, *Associate Executive Director, Program Development*

Nancy Modrak, *Director, Publishing*

John O'Neil, *Director of Acquisitions*

Julie Houtz, *Managing Editor of Books*

Carolyn R. Pool, *Associate Editor*

Charles D. Halverson, *Project Assistant*

Gary Bloom, *Director, Design and Production Services*

Karen Monaco, *Senior Designer*

Tracey A. Smith, *Production Manager*

Dina Murray, *Production Coordinator*

John Franklin, *Production Coordinator*

Cynthia Stock, *Desktop Publisher*

Robert Land, *Indexer*

ASCD publications present a variety of viewpoints. The views expressed or implied in this book should not be interpreted as official positions of the Association.

Printed in the United States of America.

December 1999 member book (p). ASCD Premium, Comprehensive, and Regular members periodically receive ASCD books as part of their membership benefits. No. FY00-3.

ASCD Stock No. 199273

Library of Congress Cataloging-in-Publication Data
Armstrong, Thomas.
    ADD/ADHD alternatives in the classroom / Thomas Armstrong.
        p. cm.
"ASCD Stock No. 199273."
Includes bibliographical references and index.
    ISBN 0-87120-359-6
    1. Attention-deficit-disordered children—Education. 2.
Attention-deficit hyperactivity disorder. I. Title.
    LC4713.2 .A76 1999
    371.93

99-006861

08 07 06 05   10 9 8 7 6 5 4

ADD/ADHD ALTERNATIVES IN THE CLASSROOM

Preface v

1
Limitations—and Assumptions—of the
ADD/ADHD Paradigm. 1

Assumption 1: ADD/ADHD is a biological disorder.. 3

Assumption 2: The primary symptoms of ADD/ADHD are
hyperactivity, distractibility, and impulsivity.. 8

Assumption 3: ADD/ADHD affects from 3 to 5 percent of all children. 10

Assumption 4: ADD/ADHD can be diagnosed through medical exams,
observation, rating scales, performance tasks, and psychological tests.. 11

Assumption 5: The most effective approach for treating ADD/ADHD
involves the administration of psychostimulants such as Ritalin.. 14

Assumption 6: Many children will continue to have ADD/ADHD
throughout their lives.. 17

Assumption 7: A child can have ADD/ADHD and also have other
disorders.. 19

2

Alternatives to the ADD/ADHD Paradigm 22

Historical Perspective 22
Sociocultural Perspective 28
Cognitive Perspective 33
Educational Perspective 35
Developmental Perspective 38
Gender Differences Perspective 42
Psychoaffective Perspective 43
Toward a Holistic Paradigm 48

3

Strategies to Empower, Not Control,
Kids Labeled ADD/ADHD 56

Educational Strategies 57
Cognitive Strategies 67
Physical Strategies 73
Affective Strategies 80
Interpersonal Strategies 87
Ecological Strategies 90
Behavioral Strategies 96
Biological Strategies 101

Epilogue 103
References 105
Index 120
About the Author 127

PREFACE

In 1962, Thomas S. Kuhn, a professor of philosophy at the Massachusetts Institute of Technology, wrote a book called *The Structure of Scientific Revolutions* that stands as one of the most significant contributions to intellectual history in the 20th century (Kuhn, 1970). In his book, Kuhn introduced the word *paradigm* as a way of talking about scientific belief systems that structure the questions, instruments, and solutions that scientists develop to explain phenomena in specific domains such as physics, chemistry, and astronomy. As a historian of science, Kuhn described how scientific belief systems change as anomalies appear in scientific research that don't seem to fit into the accepted paradigm.

For example, during the Middle Ages, scientists believed that the earth was the center of the universe, basing their conviction on the painstaking mathematical work of an Egyptian astronomer named Ptolemy, who lived in the 2nd century of the Common Era (C.E.). By the early 16th century, however, a growing number of scientists were expressing dissatisfaction with the Ptolemaic system. His paradigm was unable to account for all the motions of the heavenly bodies, and inconsistencies, or anomalies, in his system began to mount. Finally, a Polish scientist, Nicolaus Copernicus, developed a system based on viewing the earth, not as a fixed point around which every other heavenly body circulated, but as itself a body in motion around the sun. The work of Copernicus helped galvanize a scientific revolution—a paradigm shift—that fundamentally changed our view of the universe. The process of shifting paradigms was not a smooth one. Luminaries like the Italian scientist Galileo Galilei were punished by church authorities for holding to this view. Nevertheless, the Copernican paradigm won out over the Ptolemaic one, and today it is hard for a modern observer to entertain any other point of view than that of the earth as one of several planets in motion around the sun.

Over the past decade, researchers have applied Kuhn's unique view of paradigms to fields outside of science, including business (Barker, 1993), religion (Berthrong, 1994), psychology (Fuller, Walsh, & McGinley, 1997), and education (Foster, 1986). In this book, I would like to apply Kuhn's approach to the study of children, in particular, to those children who have special difficulty paying attention, concentrating, or sitting still. Over the past 20 years, a paradigm has emerged in the United States and Canada to try to explain how and why these kinds of behavior occur in certain children. The paradigm suggests that such children have something called attention-deficit-hyperactivity disorder (ADHD) or attention-deficit disorder (ADD), disorders that are said to be biological in origin, affecting from 3 to 5 percent of all children in North America. In this book, I challenge this paradigm (hereafter referred to as the ADD/ADHD paradigm) and suggest that it represents a limited and artificial way of viewing children who have difficulties with attention and behavior.

I propose that the ADD/ADHD paradigm does not adequately explain various anomalies found in the educational literature concerning children with attention and behavior difficulties. In this book, I explore other perspectives that shed light on the behavior of these children. These perspectives include historical, sociocultural, cognitive, educational, developmental, and psychoaffective domains. I do not advocate any one of these particular perspectives, but seek instead to work toward a new paradigm that incorporates aspects of each of these points of view (including the biological) within a holistic framework that addresses the needs of the whole child.

After discussing the overall framework for a new paradigm related to children with attention and behavior problems, I present many practical strategies that both regular and special education teachers can use to address the needs of children who have specific attention or behavior difficulties. These strategies span all domains of the child's world—cognitive, educational, physical, emotional, interpersonal, ecological, behavioral, and biological. It is my hope that by taking the broadest possible view of the child who struggles with attention and behavioral issues, I can help educators get out of the narrow rut of thinking engendered by the recent excessive popularity of the ADD/ADHD paradigm, and assist them in moving back to sound educational principles guiding effective practice.

THOMAS ARMSTRONG
Sonoma County, California
December 1999

LIMITATIONS—
AND ASSUMPTIONS—
OF THE ADD/ADHD PARADIGM

Over the past 20 years, a new way of thinking about children with attention and behavior problems has gained widespread acceptance from all quarters of society. I am speaking of attention-deficit disorder (ADD) or attention-deficit-hyperactivity disorder (ADHD). Sparked by recent best sellers (Hallowell & Ratey, 1994a, 1994b) and coverage by the popular press (Glusker, 1997; Hales & Hales, 1996; Machan, 1996; Wallis, 1994), ADD/ADHD has become a household term for millions of Americans. Numerous popular guides for parents and teachers have appeared explaining what ADD/ADHD is, what causes it, and how it can be diagnosed and treated (e.g., Barkley, 1995; Cohen, M. W., 1997; Green & Chee, 1998). Researchers have published thousands of scientific papers in the past 20 years on a wide range of issues related to ADD/ADHD (Resnick & McEvoy, 1994). The disorder has received the support of mainstream psychiatry (American Psychiatric Association, 1994) and general medicine (Goldman, Genel, Bezman, & Slanetz, 1998), the stamp of governmental approval (Viadero, 1991), and widespread acceptance in U.S. schools (Smallwood, 1997).

What is ADD/ADHD? Or, more properly, *What is the structure of the ADD/ADHD paradigm* or world view? Although ADD/ADHD proponents may disagree on certain matters connected with the paradigm, such as whether ADD/ADHD is overdiagnosed (e.g., Ingersoll, 1995; Gordon, 1995), many professionals, parents, and other proponents of ADD/ADHD seem to have arrived at a consensus concerning the existence of a discrete disorder (or disorders). This consensus includes several basic assumptions:

- ADD/ADHD is a biological disorder (most probably of genetic origin).
- The primary symptoms of this disorder are *hyperactivity, impulsivity,* and *distractibility.* A person can have certain of these symptoms and not others (for example, ADD doesn't include hyperactivity as a symptom, whereas ADHD does).
- This disorder affects 3–5 percent of all children and adults in the United States (and presumably the world).
- ADD/ADHD can be assessed in many ways, or in a combination of ways: a medical history; observations of the child in a variety of contexts; the use of rating scales to document these observations; performance tasks to assess such traits as vigilance; and psychological tests to assess memory, learning, and related areas of functioning.
- The most effective approaches for treating ADD/ADHD are medications and behavior modification.
- Many children will continue to have ADD/ADHD throughout their lives.
- A child can have ADD or ADHD and also have other disorders, such as learning disabilities and anxiety or mood disorders.

In this chapter, I consider each of these assumptions and describe specific anomalies in them which, when taken as a whole, tend to call into question the essential credibility of the ADD/ADHD paradigm.

Assumption 1:
ADD/ADHD is a biological disorder.

This tenet seems to be the foundation of the ADD/ADHD paradigm. To believe that ADD/ADHD is a biological disorder gives ADD/ADHD the stamp of approval of modern medicine, thus seeming to place it in a position unassailable by claims from fields with less cultural prestige, such as sociology, psychology, or education.

I'd like to focus on three major avenues of inquiry into the neurobiological basis for ADD/ADHD: positron emission tomography (PET) studies of cerebral glucose metabolism, magnetic resonance imaging (MRI) studies of structural differences between the so-called "ADHD brain" and the "normal" brain, and genetic studies.

PET Scan Studies

The single event in the history of the ADD/ADHD paradigm that garnered the greatest attention pointing to ADD/ADHD as a medical disorder was perhaps the 1990 PET scan study by A. J. Zametkin and his colleagues at the National Institute of Mental Health (NIMH) in Bethesda, Maryland (Zametkin et al., 1990). In this study, researchers injected groups of adults identified as "hyperactive" and "normal" with radioactive glucose. Researchers then tracked this substance in the brain through positron emission tomography (PET) while the subjects engaged in a simple auditory-attention task. Results indicated that the "hyperactive" group had significantly less metabolism in areas of the prefrontal lobes of the brain that were important in the control of attention and motor activity. The study received significant attention in the media as "proof" that ADD/ADHD is a medical disorder (e.g., Elmer-DeWitt, 1990; Kolata, 1990; Squires, 1990).

When Zametkin and his colleagues (1993) attempted to replicate this study with adolescents three years later, however, they failed to find any significant global differences between "hyperactive" and "normal" groups. Similarly, attempts to find differences in brain metabolism of "hyperactive" girls also yielded no significant differences (Ernst et al., 1994). As Rapoport (1995) points out, "[because] PET scans can be cumbersome and difficult to do correctly . . . it's been very hard to replicate findings."

Even if researchers were to find significant differences between the cerebral glucose metabolic rate as measured in the PET scans of so-called "normal" and "ADHD" brains, one cannot be certain that these differences result from inherent neurological problems in the ADHD groups. Recent research suggests that the environment can have a big effect on brain metabolism. Jeffrey M. Schwartz and his colleagues at UCLA School of Medicine have been able to demonstrate systematic changes in cerebral glucose metabolic rates after successful behavior modification treatment of individuals described as having obsessive-compulsive disorder (Schwartz, Stoeseel, Baxter, Martin, & Phelps, 1996). If the environment can create positive changes in cerebral glucose metabolic rates, it may also be able to create negative changes.

As the next chapter shows, factors like stress, family discord, and cultural pressures may have a large role to play in the incidence of the kinds of behavior associated with ADD/ADHD among some people. Environmental factors may well interact with brain chemistry to create what looks like an "abnormal brain" but may be instead an intact brain responding to an "abnormal environment."

MRI Studies

The use of MRI technology has allowed researchers to look at structural features in the brains of people with so-called ADD/ADHD and those of "normals." Using MRI technology, J. N. Giedd and his colleagues at NIMH compared sections of the midsagittal cross-sectional area of the corpus callosum (a collection of nerve fibers that connect right and left hemispheres) in 18 boys labeled ADHD with 18 matched "normal" boys (Giedd et al., 1994). They found that in the group identified as "ADHD," the rostrum and rostral body regions of the corpus callosum were smaller at the 0.05 level of significance.

This study, and others like it, are used as indicators that people labeled ADHD have abnormal brains. Yet the study itself stated "no gross abnormalities were found in any subject" from the MRI measurements (Giedd et al., 1994, p. 666). Moreover, the study found no correlations between brain differences and measures of attention in the people identified as "attention deficit disordered." The differences found in the "ADHD" group were subtle differences in only two of the seven regions measured—regions that relate to premotor functioning. Most important, even if these neuroanatomical differences do in fact exist (e.g., if future studies are able to replicate these findings) they could well represent just that—differences—and not necessarily disorders.

We should avoid pathologizing people so quickly, based on the subtle differences in the bumps on the inside of the brain—or we could fall into a modern-day neurological version of the trap that doctors of the 18th and 19th centuries fell into when they used facial features or bumps on the outside of the head to decide who had criminal tendencies or other unsavory moral characteristics (see Gould, 1981, for a historical perspective). To use a metaphor: If gardeners treated their flowers like psychiatrists do their "ADHD" patients, we might well hear things like "This lily has petal-deficit disorder!" or "My ivy has gone hyperactive!" We should consider the possibility that neurological diversity may be a potentially healthy development.

Genetic Studies

A third source of support for the belief that ADD/ADHD is a neurobiological disorder comes from genetic studies. In one study that received almost as much publicity as the 1990 Zametkin PET scan study described above (for an example of media attention, see Maugh, 1996), researchers at the University of California-Irvine claimed to have found a link between children with ADHD and a specific gene (the dopamine D4 receptor gene) associated with "novelty seeking" behavior (LaHoste et al., 1996).

An article that appeared in the same journal, *Molecular Biology*, a few months later (Malhatra et al., 1996), however, questioned whether there even was a link between the dopamine D4 receptor gene and the behavioral trait of novelty seeking in the first place. More recently, a follow-up article in *Molecular Biology* suggested that new data did not support an association between this gene and the brains of people identified as having ADHD (Castellanos et al., 1998).

In another study that garnered much publicity ("Hyperactive Behavior in English Schoolchildren," by Taylor & Sandberg, 1984), researchers at NIMH claimed that some cases of ADHD were due to a thyroid disorder caused by mutations in a thyroid receptor gene (Hauser et al., 1993). A follow-up study among 132 children labeled with ADHD, however, revealed no evidence of clinically significant thyroid dysfunction (Spencer, Biederman, Wilens, & Guite, 1995).

Many difficulties are inherent in attempting to build a case for a genetic basis for ADHD. First, how can one reduce the complex feelings, behaviors, and thoughts of a person to a single gene (an "ADHD" gene) or even to a series of such genes? As Harvard Professor Emeritus of Biology Ruth Hubbard explains in relation to another common educational label, learning disabilities:

> There is an enormous distance from a gene and the protein in whose synthesis it is implicated to a complex behavior like a "learning disability." Psychologists and educators need to understand this and to stop expecting practical benefits from oversimplified correlations (Hubbard & Wald, 1993, p. 129).

Second, the traits associated with ADHD are quite generalized and may look very different in different contexts. The media have variously described the dopamine D4 receptor gene as a gene for "novelty-seeking," "thrill-seeking," or "risk-taking." Each of these terms implies different things, some more positive than others. Risk-taking sounds dangerous. However, novelty-seeking may actually be a good thing. In fact, in research I describe in the next chapter, the traits of a creative person (including a penchant for novelty-seeking) look very much like the "symptoms" of ADHD. So perhaps that trait is heritable, though two studies suggest that it is not (Castellanos et al., 1998; LaHoste, 1996). But does that mean that something called "ADHD" is heritable? One must make a big leap of faith to make that connection.

Finally, genetic traits are not necessarily immutable factors hardwired into our nature from conception on. Recent research suggests that the environment may have a much larger role to play in the modification of genetic material than previously thought possible. In one study at McGill University, researchers separated newborn rats from their mothers for either 15 minutes or six hours a day. One of the researchers, biologist Michael Meaney, reported: "We found that receptors [for certain brain chemicals] and the gene for the receptors are both altered" as a result of the stress of separation in the six-hour group (Begley, 1996, p. 57).

It is quite possible, then, that stress or other environmental influences can play a wide role in the disruption of the genetic blueprint for the flow of neurotransmitters in the brains of children labeled ADD/ADHD. In such a case, it becomes problematic to say that ADD/ADHD is purely a biological or medical disorder. At best, it is more likely an intricate dance between genetic predispositions and environmental events that trigger the symptoms associated with ADD/ADHD.

Again, ADD/ADHD looks much more like a complex interaction between brain and world than any kind of intrinsic medical problem located solely inside the genes or brain chemicals of a child. Unfortunately, our culture has tended to engage in wholesale "bioreductionism" of traits and characteristics once thought to be a natural part of the spectrum of human variation. One theoretical biologist, Brian Goodwin, suggests: "We need to develop a way of doing biology by going beyond the gene and cultivating intuitive ways of knowing about wholes and about organisms" (cited in Blakeslee, 1997). The biological should be an important part of a holistic approach to children labeled ADD/ADHD, but it should not take the central reductive role that it does in the current ADD/ADHD paradigm.

Assumption 2:
The primary symptoms of ADD/ADHD are hyperactivity, distractibility, and impulsivity.

The existence of the symptoms of hyperactivity, distractibility, and impulsivity in schoolchildren is not merely a belief, it is an observed fact. To claim that these kinds of behavior represent the chief manifestations of something called ADD/ADHD, however, brings us into the realm of belief—a belief that can be questioned. This is particularly true because hyperactivity, distractibility, and impulsivity are among the most global and widespread types of behavior seen in childhood and adolescence. One can observe them in virtually all children during certain parts of their lives (especially in the early years and during adolescence), and under certain types of conditions at other stages of life that involve stress, boredom, excitement, and the like. A child can be hyperactive, distractible, or impulsive because she is depressed, anxious, allergic to milk, highly creative, bored with schoolwork, unable to read, or temperamentally difficult, among a host of other factors. How can we be precise in defining ADD/ADHD if we base identification—and labeling of children—on some combination of these three highly global kinds of behavior? What certainty exists here?

This matter is made even more uncertain when we look at studies suggesting that among children who are labeled ADD/ADHD, the symptoms of hyperactivity, distractibility, or impulsivity can decrease in intensity and even disappear in certain psychosocial contexts. Research suggests that ADD/ADHD-identified kids behave more normally in situations such as the following:

- in one-to-one relationships (see Barkley, 1990, pp. 56–57);
- in situations where they are paid to do a task (see McGuinness, 1985, p. 205);
- in environments that include novelty or high stimulation (see Zentall, 1980);
- in contexts where they can control the pace of the learning experience (Sykes, Douglas, & Morgenstern, 1973); and
- during times when they are interacting with a male authority figure rather than a female figure (Sleator & Ullmann, 1981).

Consequently, the symptoms of ADD/ADHD appear to be highly context-specific. The vagueness of the behavioral criteria used to establish a diagnosis of ADD/ADHD has led to a growing literature critical of the ADD/ADHD paradigm (e.g., Armstrong, 1997; Goodman & Poillion, 1992; McGuiness, 1989; Reid, R., Maag, & Vasa, 1993). This fuzziness will become even more apparent when we examine the assessments used to diagnose ADD/ADHD.

Assumption 3:
ADD/ADHD affects from 3 to 5 percent
of all children.

The American Psychiatric Association (1994, p. 82), in its *Diagnostic and Statistical Manual of Mental Disorders*, 4th Edition (DSM-IV), indicates that 3–5 percent of all schoolchildren have ADHD; and many sources on ADD/ADHD have followed this source (e.g., CH.A.D.D., 1994; Wallis, 1994). A wider review of the literature, however, will show quite a range of perceived variation in the incidence of ADD/ADHD. Here are some examples:

• One professional article for family physicians indicates that "the reported prevalence of this disorder in clinical practice is 6 to 8 percent" (Johnson, 1997, p. 155).

• A widely respected book on ADHD for educators reports: "It is estimated by experts that 3 to 10 percent of school-age children are affected. The estimated figures most frequently cited in the literature are 3 percent to 5 percent. However, this is very likely an underestimate due to the fact that many ADD girls go undiagnosed" (Reif, 1993, p. 3).

• Russell Barkley's comprehensive handbook on ADD/ADHD reports variations between 1 and 20 percent. He points out that any figure on the incidence of ADD/ADHD "greatly hinges on how one chooses to define ADHD, the population studied, the geographic locale of the survey, and even the degree of agreement required among parents, teachers, and professionals" (Barkley, 1990, p. 61).

Barkley's comment is telling, because it suggests that the definition of ADHD is still highly unstable and depends to a good degree on the subjective decisions of a group of people who appear not to agree with each other on what constitutes genuine ADHD (McGuinness, 1989). At one time, clinicians in the United States and Britain considered the symptoms associated with ADHD to affect only a very small proportion of the total population (less than 1 percent) (see Goodman & Poillion, 1992; Taylor & Sandberg, 1984). The past few years, however, have seen a definite "drift" toward larger and larger percentages of incidence of ADHD. Most recently, Ratey and Johnson (1998) have suggested that there may be a subclinical variety of ADHD that could extend the ADHD net over an even wider population. That ADHD should be seen as residing in a substantial proportion of the population (say, over 10 percent) when 20 years ago its existence was virtually unknown should give us pause. Could it be that the ADD/ADHD paradigm is transforming aspects of behavior that were once considered a normal part of human variation into pathological aberrations? If so, what impact is this creeping medicalization of human behavior likely to have in other spheres? Could we soon see other aspects of human variation turned into disorders (e.g., courage-deficit disorder, truth-deficit disorder, ambition-deficit disorder)?

Assumption 4:
ADD/ADHD can be diagnosed through medical exams, observations, rating scales, performance tasks, and psychological tests.

As suggested in the previous section, the variation in the numbers of people suspected of having ADD/ADHD appears to be directly related to problems with the assessments used to diagnose it. As the DSM-IV indicates: "There are no laboratory tests that have been established as diagnostic in the clinical assessment of Attention-Deficit/Hyperactivity Disorder" (American Psychiatric Association,

1994, p. 81). Consequently, professionals have had to make do with a number of methods and instruments that have had significant reliability and validity problems.

Medical Exams

What would seem to be one of the most solid approaches—an office visit to and interview with a physician trained to diagnose ADHD—appears to be one of the least successful approaches (except to rule out other possible medical problems) because research suggests that 80 percent of the time the symptoms of ADHD "disappear" in the doctor's office (Sleator & Ullmann, 1981). Reasons for this include the one-to-one relationship with a (usually) male authority in a novel environment (all factors that, as discussed in the previous section, reduce or eliminate the symptoms associated with ADD/ADHD). As a result, the assessment mainstays of ADD/ADHD diagnoses have tended to turn on two major sources of information: observations/rating scales, continuous performance tasks, and psychological testing.

Behavior Rating Scales

Behavior rating scales are typically checklists consisting of items that relate to a child's attention and behavior at home and school. In one widely used scale, teachers are asked to rate the child on a scale of 1 (almost never) to 5 (almost always) in terms of behavioral statements such as "Fidgety (hands always busy)," "Restless (squirms in seat)," and "Follows a sequence of instructions."

The main difficulty with these sorts of instruments is that they rest entirely on *subjective* judgments. How is a teacher to score a child, for example, on "Restless (squirms in seat)"? Perhaps the child squirms when required to take tests or do worksheets, but possibly not when involved in a hands-on activity. There is no room for this kind of distinction on the rating scale. Moreover, there are value judgments attached to a statement like "squirms in seat." The implication seems to be that squirming is a bad thing (e.g., leading toward a diagnosis of ADHD). But what if the child squirms due to excitement and anticipation in learning something new, or as a natural part of a highly physical nature? Moreover, whereas scales like these are focused on identifying, for example, *hyperactivity,* there should statistically speaking also be another pole on that axis that points to *hypoactivity* (the underactive child). And yet one never sees scales to identify and treat the hypoactive child. The inherent problems involved in constructing a valid scale may help explain why these scales often involve such poor agreement between groups who fill them out (McGuiness, 1985, 1989; Reid, R., & Magg, 1994).

Continuous Performance Tasks

Continuous performance tasks (CPT) appear to have resolved the problem of rating scale subjectivity by turning the assessment over to a machine (usually computerized). These tasks involve repetitive actions that require the child to remain alert and attentive throughout the test. The earliest versions of these tasks were developed to select candidates for radar operations during World War II. Their relevance to the lives of today's children seems highly tenuous.

One popular CPT instrument consists of a plastic box with a large button on the front and an electronic display above it that flashes a series of random digits. The child is told to press the button every time a "1" is followed by a "9." The box then records the number of "hits" and "misses" made by the child. Quite apart from the fact that this task bears no resemblance to anything else that the child will ever do in his life, this instrument creates an "objective" score that is taken as an important measure of his likelihood of having ADHD. Most recently, it has been used in functional magnetic resonance imaging (fMRI) studies to show differences in brain activity between children labeled ADHD and those identified as normal (Vaidya et al., 1998). In reality, it only tells us how a child will perform when forced to attend to a series of meaningless numbers on an Orwellian machine.

These types of decontextualized assessments attempt to make judgments about the whole child in terms of a tiny fraction of split-off moments of artificial experience in the life of a human being. As such, their validity—in the broadest possible sense of that word—remains highly problematic.

Psychological Tests

Educators and psychologists have used other standardized diagnostic instruments in an attempt to discriminate ADD/ADHD from non-ADD/ADHD groups, including the following:

- the Matching Familiar Figures Test (MFFT),
- certain subtest scores of the Wechsler Intelligence Scale for Children, and
- the Wisconsin Card Sort Test.

Yet even prominent figures in the ADD/ADHD world believe that such measures are misleading (e.g., Barkley, 1990, pp. 330-332).

Assumption 5:
The most effective approach for treating ADD/ADHD involves the administration of psychostimulants such as Ritalin.

Research strongly supports the effectiveness of medications such as methyphenidate hydrochloride (Ritalin) on a range of outcomes, including reduction of large and small motor movements and increased attentiveness, especially in structured, task-oriented settings such as traditional classrooms (Abikoff & Gittelman, 1985).

The medication is also associated with improvements in compliance with teacher or parent directives; reduction of aggressiveness with peers; and improved social relationships with parents, teachers, and peers (Swanson et al., 1993). If the meaning of "effective" is related to these types of outwardly observable behavioral changes, then this assumption of the ADD/ADHD paradigm could be seen as correct.

Some inherent problems with Ritalin use, however, may limit its true "effectiveness" in any deeper sense of that word. As Swanson and colleagues (1993) point out, the benefits of stimulant medications are temporary. Ritalin, for example, is a short-acting drug whose effects wear off after a few hours. Consequently, it is not by any means a "cure" or even a serious attempt to get at the root of whatever ADD/ADHD may turn out to be. It simply provides symptomatic relief.

One of the biggest problems with Ritalin is that it works so effectively. Because it quells a child's hyperactivity, impulsivity, or distractibility, parents, teachers, and professionals may be lulled into a feeling that the problem has been solved. This may keep them from attempting to use nonmedical approaches that might actually go much more deeply into the core of a child's behavioral or attentional difficulties (e.g., emotional distress, learning problems).

Ritalin also has some specific drawbacks, which many writers on the subject of ADD/ADHD have ignored or downplayed. Here are several of these disadvantages:

1. Ritalin can subtly undermine a child's sense of responsibility by causing him to attribute his positive and negative behavior to a drug (e.g., "The reason I hit that kid is that I forgot to take my 'good' pill today!") (Pelham et al., 1992; Whalen & Henker, 1980; Whalen, Henker, Hinshaw, Heller, & Huber-Dressler, 1991).

2. Although there is no clear evidence that Ritalin or other psychostimulants lead to drug abuse, it still seems imprudent to turn

immediately to a drug for a solution to life's problem, when research suggests that some kids labeled ADD/ADHD may grow up to have substance-abuse problems in adulthood (Mannuzza, Klein, Bessler, Malloy, & LaPadula, 1993). Ritalin is chemically similar—though highly different in its patterns of metabolism in the body—to cocaine (Volkow et al., 1995); and there is evidence that rats who have been exposed to Ritalin in their early development may later be more inclined to self-administer cocaine than rats who have not been previously exposed (Drug Enforcement Administration, 1995). When this information is combined with evidence that Ritalin can cause a "high" in older children and adolescence (Corrigall & Ford, 1996) and that it has been abused by teenagers as a "street drug" (Hancock, 1996; Manning, 1995), then it would seem that there is a reason not to turn automatically to Ritalin as a response to a child's hyperactive, impulsive, or distractible behavior, especially if other nonmedical approaches might work instead.

3. Research evidence shows that many children simply do not like to take drugs like Ritalin, that it makes them feel "weird," "strange," and "different from the other kids" and also provokes a number of unpleasant physical side effects, including nausea and insomnia (Sleator, Ullmann, & Neumann, 1982; Gibbs, 1998).

4. The use of psychostimulants like Ritalin can serve as a cause for disqualification from military service or participation in certain types of intercollegiate athletics (Dyment, 1990; Zoldan, 1997).

These problems certainly do not warrant the kind of backlash response among some people and groups that have viewed Ritalin use with the same kind of paranoid fervor that people used to have toward fluoridation of the water system (e.g., Cowart, 1988; Safer & Krager, 1992).

Ritalin clearly has its place in any holistic model of attention and behavior difficulties (American Academy of Pediatrics, 1987;

Turecki, 1989, p. 231). In such a context, it would appear to be a powerful tool to treat aspects of the child's difficulties that stem from biological roots.

The model I am proposing in this book, however, does not consider the biological to be the central core of the "problem" (at least for many kids labeled ADD/ADHD), but one of its many "hubs" (see Chapter 2). Thus I maintain that educators should not consider Ritalin use (and the use of other psychoactive drugs) as "the first and most effective treatment," but as one among a wide range of possible tools that educators and parents can use to help children with attention and behavioral difficulties. The difficulty with Ritalin is not that children take it, but that many professionals and parents turn to it too quickly and advocate its use with too many kids who may not actually need it when provided with access to a broader range of strategies (see Breggin, 1998; Diller, 1998; Divoky, 1989; Garber, Garber, & Spizman, 1997).

Assumption 6:
Many children will continue to have ADD/ADHD throughout their lives.

According to ADD/ADHD texts, people used to think that the symptoms associated with ADD/ADHD disappeared after childhood. However, research now suggests that some kids labeled ADD/ADHD will continue to have the "disorder" into adolescence and adulthood (American Psychiatric Association, 1994; Klein & Mannuzza, 1991). These findings have fueled a new growth industry in ADD/ADHD even greater than that originally developed around children: one geared toward the needs of the "ADD/ADHD adult" (Sudderth & Kandel, 1997).

What's missing from discussions of this new research, however, is the obvious complement to these findings: If some kids labeled

ADD/ADHD will continue to have ADD/ADHD into adulthood, it logically follows that for some kids identified as ADD/ADHD the disorder will disappear! As the DSM-IV points out:

> In most individuals, symptoms attenuate during late adolescence and adulthood, although a minority experience the full complement of symptoms of Attention-Deficit/Hyperactivity Disorder into mid-adulthood. Other adults may retain only some of the symptoms, in which case the diagnosis of Attention-Deficit/Hyperactivity Disorder, In Partial Remission, should be used (American Psychiatric Association, 1994, p. 82).

Some discussions of this subject suggest that "ADD/ADHD" kids learn to control, or compensate, or cope with their ADD/ADHD in later life. Another way of saying this is that they mature and are able to be less hyperactive, for example, or to channel that hyperactivity into appropriate social outlets.

When this type of argument is posed, however, we seem to move out of the biological paradigm—on which ADD/ADHD is based—and into a more developmental paradigm, which has different assumptions about learning and growth from those espoused by ADD/ADHD adherents (see the next chapter for a fuller discussion of a developmental perspective). Although one certainly might argue that "many children with ADD/ADHD learn to compensate for their symptoms in adulthood," one might also argue the flip side, that "people with hyperactive behavior in childhood mature and discover the value of their hyperactivity in adulthood and learn to use it to better their lives and the lives of others."

In the ADD/ADHD "half-empty glass" approach, the disorder remains into adulthood but is "minimal" or "in remission." In the more holistic/developmental "half-full glass" approach, the person grows up and, in maturing, may in fact discover that the very things that gave her so much trouble in childhood were the same traits that ultimately led to her success in adulthood!

Assumption 7:
A child can have ADD/ADHD
and also have other disorders.

This assumption that a child can have ADD/ADHD along with disorders like learning disabilities and anxiety or mood disorders includes an assumption that there are different subtypes of ADD/ADHD. This last assumption of the ADD/ADHD paradigm is the most tricky one.

As discussed earlier in this chapter, there are many problems with the definition of ADD/ADHD. As the next chapter shows, researchers have discovered many other ways of explaining hyperactivity, impulsivity, and distractibility, than by positing the existence of a discrete disorder such as ADD/ADHD. For example, the next chapter discusses how a child can be hyperactive because he is anxious or depressed, or is frustrated in learning at home and school.

How can one be certain that the hyperactivity doesn't stem from these deeper problems? ADD/ADHD experts have found a way to preserve their disorder (and thus, the entire paradigm) while explaining these anomalies at the same time. "It's simple," they might argue. "A child can be *both* ADD/ADHD and have an anxiety disorder [or a mood disorder, or a learning disability]." This sort of multiple-disorder approach is referred to as "comorbidity." Such reasoning begs the question of where the attention-deficit disorder leaves off and the anxiety disorder or learning disability begins. It allows the ADD/ADHD exponents to avoid the sticky problem of "confounding variables" (e.g., "We're not sure if it's anxiety or ADD/ADHD, so let's just say that it's both").

The same type of fractional approach has been used to deal with anomalies observed in children labeled ADD/ADHD that don't seem to fit into the original definition of an "attention deficit." For example, some parents might argue "But my child doesn't have trouble paying attention; in fact, he'll spend hours working on his Legos [or playing video games, or participating in other activities he enjoys]."

Instead of regarding this as an anomaly that challenges the foundations of the ADD/ADHD paradigm, ADD/ADHD researchers simply adjust the paradigm slightly to accommodate these new findings. "You see," they might explain to the parent, "we now know that this sort of behavior is part of the problem—we're calling it hyper-focus, and it's something that we're seeing in an increasing percentage of ADD/ADHD kids."

The very dual nature of the term itself—ADD/ADHD—reveals an attempt to cope with the observation that some kids once thought to be ADD were hyperactive, and other kids were not at all, but more distractible. Instead of using this as an opportunity to rethink the whole paradigm, the response was to retain the paradigm and simply to begin speaking of "subtypes." The proliferation of "comorbid" factors and subtypes in the ADD/ADHD world (American Psychiatric Association, 1994; Biederman, Newcorn, & Sprich, 1991; Hallowell & Ratey, 1994a, 1994b) reveals the (so far successful) attempt by ADD/ADHD proponents to preserve the paradigm in the face of growing evidence that there are many kids who simply don't fit neatly into its structure.

A paradigm can accomplish this sort of thing for only so long before it begins to break up. The 2nd century C. E. astronomer Ptolemy, for example, kept adding little epicycles to his paradigm to account for anomalies in the supposedly circular motion of the planets. Finally, the 17th century scientist Johannes Kepler accounted for the anomalies by regarding the motion of the planets as ellipses. By taking a fundamentally different perspective on looking at the motion of planets (or shifting the paradigm), Kepler was able to better account for the astronomical data then available to scientists. In the same manner, the ADD/ADHD world has attempted to account for the increasing number of anomalies in its paradigm by adding its own version of "epicycles" (e.g., subtypes, comorbid factors).

A holistic approach to the ADD/ADHD issue seeks to do away with this "add-on-the-categories" method of accounting for anomalies, and instead looks for a better way to make sense of the great diversity among kids who experience attention and behavior difficulties in the classroom. Chapter 2 explores a number of alternative paradigms or perspectives that attempt to explain this diversity in a richer way.

ALTERNATIVES TO THE ADD/ADHD PARADIGM

As I discussed in the previous chapter, the ADD/ADHD paradigm is problematic as a conceptual tool for accounting for the hyperactive, distractible, or impulsive behavior of schoolchildren. In this chapter, I'd like to explore some alternative ways of accounting for these same kinds of behavior. In essence, I present a number of competing perspectives to the biologically based, ADD/ADHD paradigm, including historical, sociocultural, cognitive, educational, developmental, gender-related, and psychoaffective perspectives. I do not argue here that any one of these paradigms should *replace* the conventional ADD/ADHD perspective as the final answer. Each of these perspectives covers *an aspect of the total picture* and includes important views that are typically left out of the ADD/ADHD world view.

Historical Perspective

Many books written from an ADD/ADHD perspective include a section that details the history of ADD/ADHD. Barkley (1990, pp. 3–38), for example, points out that ADD/ADHD was first observed in 1902 by George Still, a British physician who wrote about 20 children in his practice who were noncompliant and aggressive, and who he believed had "moral defects" due to underlying neurological problems (Still, 1902). Barkley goes on to mention an encephalitis epidemic in

1917–18 where surviving children often had ADD/ADHD-type symptoms. He then describes research during the 1930s and 1940s on the cognitive and behavioral problems of brain-damaged children and the emergence of "minimal brain damage" as a term to describe kids who had similar behavioral disturbances with no obvious brain damage. He explores the 1950s and 1960s as a time when people used the terms *hyperkinetic* and *hyperactive*; and he noted that the 1970s represented the decade of the actual birth of the term *attention-deficit disorder*. Barkley described the 1980s as a period of increasing research into ADD/ADHD and the beginnings of national advocacy efforts dedicated to treating this condition, and the 1990s as a time of further articulating the symptoms, subtypes, comorbid factors, and other features of this disorder.

The implication in this history is that ADD/ADHD has always been with us, but only in the last few years have we made real progress in our ability to track it down and treat it appropriately. It is possible, however, to take a very different view of ADD/ADHD and history. Rather than seeing the ADD/ADHD movement within the context of a biological phenomenon in the act of being historically discovered, it is possible to examine it *simply as a historical movement with its own unique life and direction.* In this context, we might see ADD/ADHD as a relatively recent phenomenon bursting on the American scene only in the last 15 years or so as a result of very specific social, political, and economic developments in psychology, psychiatry, education, business, and government.

To take an extreme position within this historical paradigm, we could regard ADD/ADHD as nothing but a historical phenomenon with very specific roots in the recent past. Even making reference to Barkley's (1990) history, until very recently, professionals in education and other related fields associated the kinds of behavior associated with ADD/ADHD with only a relatively small number of children (far less than 3–5 percent of all schoolchildren). These children thus identified had experienced very specific brain damage as a result of encephalitis, anoxia at birth, and other physical traumas or illnesses.

Since the introduction of the *Diagnostic and Statistical Manual* (DSM) by the American Psychiatric Association in 1968, professionals have shifted ADD/ADHD-like kinds of behavior from one label and diagnostic category to another. As McBurnett, Lahey, and Pfiffner (1993, p. 199) point out:

> The terminology and classification of ADD is a perplexing issue in mental health. Every new version of the DSM has included a major revision of ADD criteria. Children with the same clinical features have been given a half-dozen or so different labels. Criteria for diagnosing variants of ADD have appeared and disappeared, only to reappear again.

More tellingly, every time a redefinition appears, it seems to take in a wider number of children. Goodman and Poillion (1992) note:

> The field [of ADD] has shifted from a very narrow, medically based category to a much broader, more inclusive and more subjective category. . . . In part, this could be because the characteristics for ADD have been subjectively defined by a committee rather than having been developed on the basis of empirical evidence (p. 38).

I'd like to suggest that the explosive growth of ADD/ADHD over the past 15 years owes much to a confluence among several factors in society, including the following.

The Cognitive Revolution in Psychology

The focus of university psychologists' research agenda shifted from behaviorism (the study of external behavior) in the 1950s and early 1960s, to cognitive psychology (the study of the mind) starting in the late 1960s. Millions of dollars of research monies started to pour into studies on various cognitive components, including perception, memory, and (significantly) *attention*. By focusing research efforts on attention, it was only a matter of time before someone started to research the *absence* of attention, or "attention deficits." In a sense, attention-deficit disorder was "cooked up" as a legitimate concept in the psychological research facilities of the United States and Canada because of this change in research priorities.

The Psychobiological Revolution in Psychiatry

Psychiatry went through a similar type of shift in priorities by turning its focus of attention from psychoanalysis in the 1930s–1950s to psychobiology starting in the 1950s–1960s. Instead of regarding a child's hyperactivity as due to a father complex in need of years of analysis, psychiatrists now were more inclined to regard it as a psychobiological problem needing a psychopharmaceutical treatment. This change in direction was an important influence in a concomitant surge in the growth of new psychoactive drugs supported by a multibillion-dollar pharmaceutical industry.

Parent Advocacy and Legislative Support

Starting in the early 1960s, parents began to organize politically to have their underachieving children identified as having a "problem" that would be recognized by medical and legislative authority. The Association for Children with Learning Disabilities (ACLD), for example, was founded in 1964 and started to lobby the U.S. Congress for special status for children identified as "learning disabled." In 1968, this effort succeeded in having learning disabilities (LD) listed as a handicapping condition by the U.S. Government, and in 1975, in helping to ensure school services for this disability under Public

Law 94-142, the Education for All Handicapped Children Act (Lynn, 1979; Sigmon, 1987).

Similar parental political involvement in the ADD/ADHD arena achieved a milestone with the founding of Children and Adults with Attention Deficit Disorders (CH.A.D.D.) in 1987. Curiously, however, parents' efforts to have ADD/ADHD legislatively approved as a handicapping condition was thwarted in 1990; Congress refused to list ADD/ADHD as a handicapping condition under new special education laws (Moses, 1990b).

ADD/ADHD, however, did receive tacit legislative support through a 1991 U.S. Department of Education letter to chief state school officers explaining how ADD/ADHD services could be obtained through existing federal laws (R. R. Davila, M. L. Williams, & J. T. MacDonald, personal communication (memo), September 16, 1991; Moses, 1991). As a result of this approval, people identified as having ADD/ADHD became eligible for specific benefits, including extra time in taking high-stakes tests like the Medical College Admissions Test (MCAT), Social Security money to families with an "ADD/ADHD" child, and other school and work accommodations (Machan, 1996).

A Boom in Privately Marketed Merchandise

ADD/ADHD has become a veritable growth industry and an important new economic market for hundreds of educational manufacturers, testing companies, publishers, entrepreneurs, and other individuals and organizations with books, kits, tests, devices, herbal remedies, training, and other tools and services to help the "ADD/ADHD child." The healthy U.S. economic boom during the 1990s has helped to support this industry, which through its own advertising and advocacy continues to put pressure on consumers to keep this market alive and growing into the future (A.D.D. Warehouse, 1998; Glusker, 1997).

Attention from the Popular Media

As noted in Chapter 1, over the past five years attention-deficit disorder (and its chief treatment, Ritalin) have moved out of the strictly psychoeducational domain and into the popular culture through the publication of such best-sellers as *Driven to Distraction* (Hallowell & Ratey, 1994a), cover stories in magazines such as *Time* and *Newsweek* (Hancock, 1996; Gibbs, 1998; Wallis, 1994), and national TV time on "Oprah" and other talk shows. This mass media attention has led to greater awareness and demand among parents for identification and services for their children and thus has fueled a new surge in the ADD phenomenon.

Naturally, one might argue that each of these historical developments merely reflects our society's growing awareness of a real disorder. On the other hand, one might consider what the nature of the ADD/ADHD phenomenon would be today if any combination of the following scenarios had happened in the past 30 years:

• Psychology had decided to focus on the study of the *volition* instead of *cognition* (we might instead have WDD or "will-deficit disorder"!)

• Psychiatry had turned to Chinese medicine instead of psychobiology for a treatment for "hyperactivity" (we might be using acupuncture instead of Ritalin as a treatment).

• The U.S. Department of Education had *not* sent a letter to chief school officers in the 50 states in 1991 legitimizing ADD/ADHD (ADD might well have been dead in the water, administratively speaking, in our classrooms).

- ADD/ADHD had remained an obscure academic construct restricted to psychology departments without any attention in the popular media or without highly active parent advocate groups pressing for services (ADD services might simply have cropped up in a few "laboratory" classrooms around the country).

In short, then, I'd like to suggest that ADD/ADHD has become a national phenomenon that appears to have taken on a life of its own. Many different parts of society have come together to fuel this phenomenon. There is no conspiracy here, but rather a confluence of parties who all appear to gain something from the arrangement:

- Psychologists receive research funds for new studies.
- Psychiatrists get new clients and have new treatment options.
- Parents gain recognition that their children's problems aren't due to poor parenting or bratty behavior.
- Entrepreneurs create new economic markets for books, materials, tests, and services.
- Politicians get votes for supporting legislation for "handicapped children" (a veritable political plum when election time rolls around).
- The popular media have "angles" for stories on a hot new topic.

I'm not suggesting that ADD/ADHD is *only* a historical movement supported by the political and economic agendas, but I would suggest that any account that attempts to leave the "phenomena of ADD/ADHD" out of the big picture would be surely lacking in completeness.

Sociocultural Perspective

Although the preceding historical analysis certainly reflects a sociocultural perspective, I'd like to go more deeply into the possible social or cultural reasons that a society like ours may need to have a label like ADD/ADHD. When parent advocacy groups began to press for special education services for their underserved kids in the 1960s, our society was changing in ways that may help explain why so many parents became concerned with their noncompliant, unmotivated, and academically frustrated kids.

The decade of the 1960s marks a watershed period in American life when social turmoil (highlighted by the Civil Rights Movement and the Vietnam War) served to shake up many previously sacrosanct institutions, including the family. In the past 30 years, the American family has undergone a significant fragmentation. There are twice as many single-parent households—8 million—as there were in 1970. The number of working mothers has risen 65 percent from 10.2 million in 1970 to 16.8 million in 1990. As Harvard professor Lester Grinspoon and Susan B. Singer observed in the *Harvard Educational Review* in 1973,

> Our society has been undergoing a critical upheaval in values. Children growing up in the past decade have seen claims to authority and existing institutions questioned as an everyday occurrence. . . . Teachers no longer have the unquestioned authority they once had in the classroom. . . . The child, on the other side, is no longer so intimidated by whatever authority the teacher has (pp. 546–547).

Grinspoon and Singer point out that "hyperkinesis [a term used to describe ADD symptoms in the 1960s and early 1970s], whatever organic condition it may legitimately refer to, has become a convenient label with which to dismiss this phenomenon as a physical 'disease' rather than treating it as the social problem it is." Attention-deficit disorder, then, may in large part be a reflection of a societal breakdown in values. To consider it simply as a "neurological disorder" is to ignore the broader social framework within which these symptoms occur (for other social critiques around this time, see Block, 1977; Conrad, 1975; Schrag & Divoky, 1975).

Another social factor over the past 30 years is the emergence of fast-paced popular media—especially television. After the early beginnings of television in the late 1940s and 1950s, the medium soon became highly sophisticated in "grabbing the attention" of its viewers to garner high ratings and sell products. In fact, millions of dollars were spent by advertisers and programmers in mastering techniques that would essentially modify the attention of its viewers: bright colors; loud sounds; catchy jingles; and, most of all, rapidly changing images. Over time, advertisers learned that viewers would habituate to a certain pace and method of presentation and would need something newer and faster to hold their attention. Consequently, commercials and programming have gotten faster and faster over the past 30 years.

Compare, for example, the number of camera shifts in an episode of "I Love Lucy" to any current comedy or drama. This shift in images becomes even more apparent in the arena of video games, music videos, and other more recent media fare. We seem to be living in a "short attention span culture" where information is served up in quick bites rather than longer and more thoughtful episodes. Witness the attempt by CBS News in the 1992 election, for example, to provide "more coverage" to political speeches (Berke, 1992). They experimented with 30-second "sound bites" but discovered that was too long for the average adult attention span, and so they went back to the industry standard of seven seconds! If this is true of the average adult, then what about the youngster who has been raised on MTV, computer games, and the Internet? In this sense, then, ADD/ADHD-like symptoms in epidemic numbers may represent less a biological disorder than a natural outcome of our children's brains being reprogrammed by short-attention-span popular media (Healy, 1991, 1998).

In this broader sociocultural perspective, it also becomes possible to argue that society may have actually needed to construct a concept such as "attention-deficit disorder" to help *preserve* some of those traditional values that appear to be falling apart. The social theorist Ivan Illich (1976) once wrote: "Each civilization defines its own diseases. What is sickness in one might be chromosomal abnormality, crime, holiness or sin in another" (p. 112). These definitions become even more urgent when children are involved.

As former American Psychological Association president Nicholas Hobbs (1975) once put it: "A good case can be made for the position that protection of the community is a primary function of classifying and labeling children who are different or deviant" (p. 20). He suggested that the Protestant work ethic, for example, may represent a set of values needing protection in our country. He writes: "According to this doctrine . . . God's chosen ones are inspired to attain to positions of wealth and power through the rational and efficient use of their time and energy, through their willingness to control distracting impulses, and to delay gratification in the service of productivity, and through their thriftiness and ambition" (p. 24). Such a society might well be expected to define deviance in terms of factors that are in opposition to these values, for example, distractibility, impulsiveness, lack of motivation, and other traits that find their way into the medical literature as symptoms of ADD/ADHD.

To be blind to the impact of these broader social contexts in the labeling of children as ADD/ADHD is to court potential disaster and to invite the ridicule of future generations. An illustration of this kind of 20/20 hindsight comes to us from pre-Civil War American medicine. In the 1850s, a Louisiana medical doctor, Samuel Cartwright, proposed a new medical disorder in the *New Orleans Medical and Surgical Journal* called *drapetomania* (Cartwright, 1851). This word essentially means "a mania for running away." He felt that *drapetomania* afflicted large numbers of runaway slaves and that, with proper identification and treatment, these slaves could learn to live productive lives back on the plantations!

As recently as the 1930s, psychiatrists classified individuals who scored poorly on intelligence tests as "morons," "imbeciles," and "idiots" (Gould, 1981). What will future generations say in looking back on our propensity for labeling millions of American schoolchildren as "attention-deficit hyperactivity disordered"?

The cultural loading involved in the term *attention-deficit hyperactivity disorder* can also be seen in cross-cultural studies on ADD/ADHD. In one study, psychiatrists from four different cultures were asked to look at a videotape of a child and determine if the child was hyperactive. Chinese and Indonesian clinicians gave significantly higher scores for hyperactive-disruptive behavior than did their Japanese and American counterparts (Mann, E. M. et al., 1992). In another study in Britain, only .09 percent of schoolchildren were identified as hyperactive (Taylor & Sandberg, 1984).

Other studies have examined similar discrepancies between cultures in the perception of ADD/ADHD-type behavior (see Furman, 1996; Reid, R., & Maag, 1997). Orlick (1982) relates parental attitudes in North America with those held in Papua, New Guinea: "If I take my daughter out to eat in North America, she is expected to sit quietly and wait (like an adult) even if there are all kinds of interesting objects and areas and people to explore. . . . Now if I take her out to a village feast in Papua New Guinea, none of these restrictions are placed on her. The villagers don't expect children to sit quietly for an hour while orders are taken and adults chat" (p. 128). Certainly, this is no prescription to let children run amok in American restaurants, but it does point to how different cultural contexts have different sorts of expectations for behavior and attention, and that educators need to be sensitive to the differences that may exist between "school culture" and the indigenous cultures of kids—especially those who are at risk to be labeled (Hartocollis, 1998).

Cognitive Perspective

Even though the ADD/ADHD paradigm has emerged in part from a cognitive focus on "attention," we can also use the cognitive approach to reach different conclusions. To put it another way, we might find it productive to spend less time exploring cognitive deficits as a medical disorder, and more time looking at the positive side of how some children labeled ADD or ADHD deploy their attention or use their minds. Some research, in fact, suggests that many children labeled ADD or ADHD are very good at paying attention: paying attention to what they're not supposed to be paying attention to! Sometimes this is referred to as "incidental attention" (e.g., instead of focusing on the teacher's voice or textbook page, they scan the walls, listen to voices in the halls, and daydream about what they'd rather be doing). Research suggests that children labeled ADD or ADHD may use incidental attention in cognitive processing and possess a more diffused or global attentional style (Ceci & Tishman, 1984; Fleisher, Soodak, & Jelin, 1984).

The finding of "global attention" raises another more fundamental cognitive issue: the relationship between the symptoms of ADD/ADHD and the traits of a creative person. For if we characterize the "ADD/ADHD child" as having a mind that does not stay still, but rather focuses on whatever interests it, and does this in a highly idiosyncratic and global way, then we are moving very close to a style of mind that appears to characterize the creative person. As Cramond (1994) suggests, if one lines up the symptoms of ADD/ADHD with the traits of creative people, there are some striking similarities. Both groups tend to daydream, shift activities frequently, have trouble complying with authority, have high activity levels, take chances, act spontaneously, and generally walk to the beat of a different drummer.

Could it be that we are pathologizing creative behavior by describing it as ADD/ADHD? This is a matter well worth taking seriously because societies have historically been notorious in failing to recognize creative people for their positive contributions (see Neumann, 1971). Over the past two thousand years, creative individuals have been burned, crucified, imprisoned, put under house arrest, exiled, and more recently medicated, to mention only a few methods by which society seeks to repress any force that might threaten to change its structure.

Some ADD/ADHD advocates might point out that creative people can be differentiated from people with ADD/ADHD by their fruits, in other words, by the way that they fashion products and solve problems in novel ways; that the ADD/ADHD individual fails to do this, and quite to the contrary has significant difficulty solving problems, fashioning worthy products, or engaging in other successful endeavors. This position, however, is weakened by the lack of research in the ADD/ADHD community on whether people labeled ADD or ADHD are in fact creative or not. There is evidence to suggest that many of them are (Berlin, 1989; Cramond, 1994; Hartmann, 1997; O'Neill, 1994; Shaw & Brown, 1991; Weiss, 1997; Zentall, 1988).

Interestingly, Hallowell and Ratey (1994a) have acknowledged that many people labeled ADD/ADHD are creative and have incorporated this fact into the ADD/ADHD paradigm by speaking about a "creative subtype" of ADD/ADHD. As mentioned in the previous chapter, this use of subtyping effectively resolves some troubling issues within the ADD/ADHD paradigm—in this case, suggesting that there is no dilemma about whether we are confusing creativity traits with ADD/ADHD symptoms, for a person can have both. This preserves the ADD/ADHD paradigm. I'd like to suggest, however, that we can just as easily leave this matter open to question and challenge the ADD/ADHD paradigm by suggesting that at least some of the children we are diagnosing as ADD/ADHD might be much better seen as primarily creative individuals.

Of course, another ADD/ADHD retort might be that some children are, in fact, misdiagnosed as ADD/ADHD who are actually highly creative, but this also dodges the central issue of whether the paradigm in the first place has contributed to this confusion. Certainly to help answer this question, educators need to dust off their creativity instruments and develop new assessments of creativity that allow us to better observe creative abilities in children who have been labeled ADD or ADHD.

Educational Perspective

One of the most troubling aspects of the rise of ADD/ADHD labeling in our schools is that it represents an incursion of the medical or biological paradigm into an arena that was previously the domain of educators. Previously, if a child were having trouble paying attention, a teacher's training would guide the teacher to ask questions like these:

- How does this child learn best?
- What kind of learning environment should I create for him to bring out his natural learning abilities?
- How can I change my lessons to gain his attention?

The focus of the teacher would be on understanding the child as a learner, and being able to make choices about structuring the educational environment through instructional strategies, teaching methods, educational tools and resources, programmatic changes, and the like.

Now, with the predominance of the biological paradigm in today's world, a teacher is more likely to ask questions like: "Does this child have ADD or ADHD?" "Should I have him tested?" "Would medication help?" and other questions that would serve to shift the teacher away from her crucial function as an educator. The practitioners of the biological paradigm are not particularly interested in determining the preferred learning style of a hyperactive, impulsive, or distractible child. They simply want to determine a diagnosis of ADD/ADHD and then treat the disorder.

A review of the literature on ADD/ADHD reveals virtually no information about the ways in which kids labeled ADD or ADHD actually learn best, their preferred learning or thinking styles, their most highly developed multiple intelligences, or their best modes of cognitive expression. When they do take up the question of learning style, it is usually couched in a negative context: "Is there the comorbid factor of learning disabilities additionally present in this child?" (Barkley, 1990, pp. 75–77). People continue to ask this despite the view of some authorities that in many cases it may be *difficulties with learning* that are causing a child's attention or behavior problems in the first place (McGee & Share, 1988).

What *is* clear, however, is that the learning environment that students labeled ADD/ADHD seem to have the hardest time with is the standard American classroom. In many other learning environments, so-called ADD/ADHD kids have far less difficulty, and even thrive. Here are some examples: an art studio, a wood shop, a dance floor, or the outdoors. As one of the nation's leading authorities on ADD/ADHD, Russell Barkley, put it when referring to such kids: "The classroom is their Waterloo" (Moses, 1990a, p. 34). What Barkley is speaking of here is the *traditional* American classroom: straight desks, teacher lecturing at the front of the room, textbooks and worksheets, and lots of listening, waiting, following directions, and reading and writing.

In classroom learning environments where kids labeled hyperactive or ADHD have the opportunity to engage in movement, hands-on learning, cooperative learning, arts education, project-based learning, or other innovative designs, their behavior is much less likely to be problematic (Eddowes, Aldridge, & Culpepper, 1994; Jacob, O'Leary, & Rosenblad, 1978; Zentall, 1980, 1993a).

Zentall (1993a), in hypothesizing that kids labeled ADHD require higher levels of stimulation than the average person, has experimented with creating high-stimulation classrooms (music, color, activity) that seem to lower the levels of hyperactivity in groups of elementary-age boys. In a sense, she is creating the equivalent of "educational Ritalin" by providing stimulation in the form of an interesting classroom environment.

The theory of multiple intelligences provides an excellent model for viewing the behavior of a child labeled ADHD (Long & Bowen, 1995). Gardner (1983, 1993) suggests that our concept of intelligence, based on IQ testing, is far too limited and needs to be replaced with a model that includes many kinds of intelligences. He has thus far established the existence of eight intelligences: linguistic, logical-mathematical, spatial, musical, bodily-kinesthetic, interpersonal, intrapersonal, and naturalist. He suggests that our schools focus too much attention on linguistic and logical-mathematical intelligences at the expense of recognizing and nurturing the other six intelligences. I have suggested in my own writings (Armstrong, 1987a, 1987b, 1988, 1994, 1997) that children with school labels like LD and ADD/ADHD may have difficulties paying attention in school because their own most highly developed intelligences are being neglected.

For example, a child who is highly bodily-kinesthetic—who needs to learn by moving, touching, and building things—would be at a distinct disadvantage in a classroom where there are no hands-on, dynamic, interactive activities. Highly physical learners who must sit quietly for hours a day engaged in small motor tasks like writing and reading are likely to feel highly frustrated, experience their attention wandering frequently, and find themselves moving in their seats in a way that could be easily interpreted as ADD/ADHD by a teacher inclined toward that paradigm.

Similarly, kids with strengths in the naturalist intelligence may feel stifled if there is nothing in the environment to stimulate their love of the natural world; kids with a strong spatial intelligence may tune out easily if the environment lacks any use of pictures and images to teach basic subjects; and a curriculum based on individualized learning may frustrate the child who requires a social context to learn most effectively.

Similarly, other theories about how kids learn suggest that the symptoms of ADD/ADHD may result from a disjunction between the way a child learns best and the environment available to her (Dunn, R., personal communication, 1994; Yelich & Salamone, 1994).

Fortunately, school-study teams and other institutional structures are using these kinds of educational models to generate solutions to help kids with attention or learning problems stay out of the special education system. If more teachers were to first ask educational questions ("How can I help him learn better?") rather than turning immediately to the more biological questions ("Does he have ADD/ADHD?"), education would benefit through the introduction of a greater variety of teaching methods, and the child would benefit from experiencing success in a regular classroom environment.

Developmental Perspective

As I pointed out in Chapter 1 of this book, a key tenet of the ADD/ADHD paradigm—that some kids with ADD/ADHD will continue to have it in adulthood—can just as easily imply its opposite: that in some cases, ADD/ADHD will go "into remission," become minimal, or even disappear as these kids mature. One recent study suggests that the rate of ADHD in any given age group appears to decline by 50 percent approximately every five years. Thus, assuming an ADHD prevalence rate of 4 percent in childhood, the estimated rate of adult ADHD would be 0.8 percent at age 20 and 0.05 percent at age 40 (Hill & Schoener, 1996). This more sanguine perspective suggests that for many kids, a developmental paradigm may be a better way of accounting for their behavior than a biological one.

Before the ADD/ADHD paradigm was so popular on the cultural scene, a rambunctious child brought to a physician might be told: "Don't worry, he'll grow out of it!" Clearly, such a prescription, in the absence of any other supportive measures, can easily serve as a cop-out or a way of ignoring serious problems that may linger underneath the surface. For some kids, however, this type of prescription worked. As they had more experiences in life, received feedback from others, and acquired more life skills and self-control, many kids did in fact settle down, perhaps not entirely, but enough to be able to function well in the adult world.

I recall a student whom I taught in a special education program at the elementary school level showing up years later in one of my regular college courses on child development. I could see that the hyperactive behavior from his childhood was still there, but it had changed—mostly this kind of behavior had gone "underground" as small motor movements that were scarcely observable. This is, in fact, what happens to most of us.

As young children, we all had the classic warning signs of ADD/ADHD: hyperactivity, distractibility, and impulsivity! Over time, we learned to inhibit some of these behaviors; but in many other cases, we simply learned to *minimize* or *internalize* them to the extent that they would no longer be problematic in social situations. The restless arms and legs in childhood became an index finger tapping faintly on the table or a leg jiggling under the office desk in adulthood. Moreover, we learned to use thought and its accoutrements (words, images, etc.) to help us do in maturity what our motor activity used to accomplish in childhood. So, instead of flailing out in anger at a rude person, as we might have done in early childhood, we simply mutter to ourselves "That guy is a jerk!" in adulthood. This is maturity!

The ability to accomplish these various skills has its biological underpinnings in the myelinization (or "sheathing") of neuronal connections as we grow up (Diamond & Hopson, 1998). Although people reach certain milestones at certain ages, the process of development (sensorimotor, cognitive, social, and biological) is an individual one—different people mature at different rates. One of the biggest problems with the ADD/ADHD paradigm is that it seems relatively insensitive to these developmental variations.

I sometimes wonder what Jean Piaget would have said about ADD/ADHD had it been around during his lifetime. I expect that if he were asked about it, he might call it an "American problem" just as he did when asked by American educators how to go about getting kids to move more quickly through his developmental stages (Duckworth, 1979). My guess is that he would have regarded ADD/ADHD symptoms as a normal reaction on the part of the child to environmental influences that were not in synch with his or her developmental level.

This raises the possibility that *developmentally inappropriate* practices may represent another contributory factor to the appearance of ADD/ADHD over the past 20 years. As David Elkind (1981, 1984, 1988) and others have pointed out, we seem to be pushing all of our kids to grow up too quickly, moving them through developmental stages before they're ready to leave them. Tasks that were once expected to be mastered by first graders are now expected to be achieved in kindergarten. Kindergarten skills are moved back to pre-school (Moses-Zirkes, 1992). I've heard preschool teachers say to me, "You know, I'd like to let my kids do more free play, puppets, painting, and dress-up, but I feel I have to use the overhead and these worksheets to get them ready for kindergarten, where it gets really rough!"

This cultural trend toward speeding up development (Piaget's original "American problem") may cause parents and educators to have unrealistic expectations for some children. Louise Bates Ames (1985) wrote of a *56-week-old boy* who had been seen by her clinic after a previous evaluator had described him as a possibly future "learning disabled child with emotional problems" because he had thrown objects and didn't seem to concentrate! If we would simply let children be children, we might find less need to regard some kids' behavior as ADD/ADHD. More relaxed developmental expectations would also lessen the pressure on kids who are feeling pushed by parents or teachers, and this could directly result in a lessening of the behavior of hyperactivity, distractibility, and impulsivity.

One last reflection that I'd like to make on developmental issues concerns the fact that in many cases, the so-called developmental immaturity seen in many kids labeled ADD/ADHD may in fact be a *positive* thing. In the field of evolutionary studies, there is a concept called *neoteny* (a Latin word that means "holding youth"), which suggests that as species evolve, there is more and more of a tendency for youthful traits to be held into adulthood (see Gould, 1975). For example, the forehead and chin of a young chimpanzee appear very humanlike. But as that chimp grows into adulthood, those traits are lost: the forehead juts out sharply and the chin recedes. In these cases, neoteny does *not* hold true; those two youthful traits are not held into adulthood. But in the human being, we see how the young child's forehead and chin are "carried through" into adulthood more or less intact structurally. The more that species evolve, the more one finds examples of neoteny present. Montagu (1983) has suggested that there are youthful *psychological* characteristics (such as creativity, spontaneity, and curiosity) that need to be "held" into adulthood in order to help our species evolve.

It appears that many kids labeled ADD/ADHD have these child-like traits. Some of these kids are still like toddlers in some ways—moving toward whatever catches their interest, blurting out very unusual perceptions, showing spontaneity in their actions. We should be careful not to put a negative connotation (implied by the term "developmentally immature") on this type of behavior. Carefully nurtured and channeled, these types of behavior can form the basis for later mature creativity. One thinks of someone like Winston Churchill, who was an absolute terror in childhood—a major behavior problem—who managed to take that frantic kid energy and transmute it over time into a channeled intensity that won him the Nobel Prize for Literature and helped save the world from tyranny.

Gender Differences Perspective

One of the most consistent findings in the field of ADD/ADHD is the preponderance of boys over girls among diagnoses made. ADHD diagnoses occur at a ratio of anywhere from 4:1 to 9:1 (boys to girls) (American Psychiatric Association, 1994). Why is this so? I'd like to suggest that studies of *normal gender differences* can help explain these disparities.

In studies of "normal" children engaged in free play, McGuinness (1985) observed that boys spent less time on any given activity (8 minutes for boys, 12 minutes for girls) and changed activities three times more frequently than girls. This kind of male-identified penchant for continuous change will be obvious to any family that has a remote control device for changing channels on their TV set! More-over, McGuinness reviewed other research on gender differences and suggested that overall, boys tend to focus more on hands-on object-play (playing with action figures, miniature vehicles, blocks), whereas girls are more likely to engage in social interactions. Finally, McGuinness noted that girls are more sensitive to, and able to differentiate, subtle verbal sounds, and boys are more attuned to nonverbal sounds (such as the fire engine passing by, or the sound of footsteps in the hall).

Each of these normal gender differences tends to favor girls in a traditional classroom setting where a usually female teacher (at the elementary school level) presides over a setting that encourages per-sistence on academic tasks, social cooperation, and attention to the verbal sounds of the teacher's voice. Conversely, the normal gender differences of boys—wanting to change activities more frequently, seeking to engage in hands-on experiences, focusing more on nonver-bal stimuli—are likely to be seen as hyperactivity, impulsivity, and distractibility—the three key "symptoms" of ADHD. David Elkind suggests that many boys are being labeled as ADHD who, 30 years ago, would have been considered as simply displaying "all boy" behav-ior (Elkind, personal communication, 1996). *Forbes* magazine sug-gested that if American society had a stronger "male liberation movement," such gross mislabeling of normal male behavior would never be tolerated (Machan, 1996; see also Robinson, 1998).

Psychoaffective Perspective

A final alternative paradigm relates to the psychoaffective dimensions of the child's life, including the influence of psychological trauma, family dynamics, and personality factors in giving rise to the behavior of hyperactivity, distractibility, and impulsivity. Strong emotions in a child—anger, frustration, sadness, fear—can quite easily produce these and related kinds of behavior. There is a body of research suggesting that as many as 25 percent of children labeled ADD/ADHD suffer from severe anxiety, and that up to 75 percent of ADD/ADHD-identified children may have some form of depression (Biederman et al., 1991).

As discussed earlier, these emotional problems are usually described in the ADD/ADHD world as "comorbid factors" accompanying ADD/ADHD (e.g., a child can have ADD/ADHD and have an anxiety disorder and/or a mood disorder etc.). However, this begs the question of whether the ADD/ADHD symptoms *may actually be due* to these deeper emotional problems. In a psychodynamic paradigm, a child who has suffered emotional trauma (e.g., divorce, illness, violence, or sexual or physical abuse), may repress the emotional pain and act it out through hyperactivity, impulsivity, distractibility, aggression toward others, and related kinds of behavior. There is a growing body of research suggesting that such traumas can actually impair neurobiological functioning (Arnsten, 1999; Perry & Pollard, 1998).

The danger with the current popularity of the ADD/ADHD paradigm is that parents, teachers, and physicians might tend to gravitate toward the more superficial but popular diagnosis of ADD/ADHD, and medicate it away with short-acting Ritalin (the pharmaceutical equivalent of a behavioral Band Aid), rather than investigate the possibility of a more serious emotional disorder—one that may be significantly more difficult to treat, more expensive to treat (a problem for short-term, managed care approaches to treatment), and far less socially palatable (few parents want their kids labeled as "emotionally disturbed," whereas the ADD/ADHD label is much more acceptable). Ritalin may have the effect of reducing or even eliminating the surface behavior problem, while the emotional disturbance continues to lurk underneath the surface of the child's psyche.

One of the biggest problems with the ADD/ADHD paradigm is that it reflects a rather limited understanding of the human psyche.

There is virtually no reference in the ADD/ADHD literature to the important contributions of thinkers like Sigmund Freud, Carl Jung, Alfred Adler, and Erik Erikson to an understanding of children's behavior. One finds in the ADD/ADHD literature, on the contrary, statements that appear to discount psychotherapeutic approaches to hyperactivity. For example, Ingersoll (1988) comments:

> Since . . . current evidence indicates that the hyperactive child's difficulties are caused by physical malfunctions in the brain, it makes little sense to look to psychological methods for relief. And in fact, there is simply no convincing evidence that psychotherapy helps to alleviate the hyperactive child's inattentiveness, poor impulse control, or motor hyperactivity (p. 92).

However, Ross and Ross (1982) write: "Traditional psychotherapy was firmly rejected as a part of the treatment armamentarium for hyperactivity, the major basis for this drastic stance being one methodologically inadequate study" (p. 7). Consequently, the impact of the human unconscious on behavior such as hyperactivity and distractibility, the role of the ego in mediating strong emotions involved in impulsivity, and other important psychodynamic issues, have been essentially left out of their research. Yet there *are* good examples in the clinical literature investigating psychodynamic issues in children whose outer turbulent behavior suggests intense inner conflict (see, e.g., Dreikurs & Soltz, 1964; Erikson, 1977, pp. 33–34; Jung, 1981; Nylund & Corsiglia, 1997; Tyson, 1991).

Another psychodynamic approach that receives very little attention from traditional ADD/ADHD researchers is that of family systems. In family systems theory, each member of the family is seen as a part of an interconnected whole, and each member influences and is influenced by every other person in the family. Problems that develop in individual family members are not seen as residing "within" that individual but rather as emerging from difficulties in the entire family system (Goldenberg & Goldenberg, 1980; Napier & Whitaker, 1988; Satir, 1983). In this context, a child who is restless and distractible may well be acting out problems that exist between parents, playing out conflicts with sibling, or even responding to conflicts going back more than two generations (McGoldrick & Gerson, 1986). To identify one particular child as having the problem is considered by some family systems practitioners to be a form of "scapegoating" (Christensen, Phillips, Glasgow, & Johnson, 1983). Putting the problem onto one family member often makes it easier for other members of the family to avoid dealing with their own issues.

Studies suggest that children identified as ADD/ADHD are more likely to come from families where there is marital distress, parental anxiety and depression, and other familial stresses (Carlson, Jacobvitz, & Sroufe, 1995; Diller & Tanner, 1996). So it is not far-fetched to suggest that some kids may buckle under the weight of these disturbed family dynamics. Not surprisingly, most ADD/ADHD theorists vigorously deny these influences and suggest instead the role of genetics, and also the disturbing influence of the ADD/ADHD-labeled child on the family—which in the context of family systems theory would be a particularly wholesale form of scapegoating (see Biederman et al., 1995).

A final psychological interpretation of an ADD/ADHD-identified child's behavior comes to us from temperament studies. Psychologists have observed for decades that children come into life with already existing personality styles or temperaments that strongly influence them throughout their lives. One particular theory developed by Stella Chess and Alexander Thomas at New York University suggests that children are born with one of three possible temperaments: the easy child, the slow-to-warm child, and the difficult child (Chess & Thomas, 1996).

New York psychiatrist Stanley Turecki (1989, 1995) has spent a great deal of time researching the traits of the *difficult child* and has suggested that difficult children possess combinations of some of the following nine characteristics: high activity level, distractibility, high intensity, irregularity, negative persistence, low sensory threshold, initial withdrawal, poor adaptability, and negative mood (see also Greenspan, 1996). Many of these kinds of behavior describe children who have been labeled as ADD/ADHD. Interestingly, Turecki considers "the difficult child" as a *normal* child (he believes that up to 20 percent of all children possess this temperament). As he points out:

> I strongly believe that you don't have to be average in order to be normal. Nor are you abnormal simply because you are difficult. . . . Human beings are all different, and a great variety of characteristics and behaviors falls well into the range of normality (Turecki, 1989, p. 18).

Temperament researchers suggest that the biggest problem for difficult children is when they are born to parents who have difficulties adapting to their child's temperament, and there results what is called a lack of "goodness of fit." In this sense, the symptoms of ADD/ADHD could be regarded (in a way similar to family systems theory) as not within the child *per se*, but rather in the "lack of chemistry" between parent and child. As Cameron (1978) observes: "Behavioral problems resembled metaphorically the origins of earthquakes, with children's temperament analogous to the fault lines, and environmental events, particularly parenting styles, analogous to strain" (p. 146).

Turecki's remarks cited previously also reveal a broader and more significant issue regarding human variation. He suggests that *normal* human behavior exists along a broad spectrum of energy levels, moods, and degrees of sociability. Educators have to be very careful that they do not define this behavioral spectrum too narrowly. A holistic approach to the ADD/ADHD issue would include a healthy respect for human diversity and a reticence to pathologize human beings who simply march to the beat of a different drummer.

Toward a Holistic Paradigm

In considering all the paradigms discussed here, you may find many different ways to think about the question of ADD/ADHD and a diversity of perspectives that educators can take toward children who have that label. Simply viewing the child through the lens of a biological paradigm is not enough. We must see the whole child against the backdrop of his physiology, personality, gender, developmental level, learning styles, educational and cultural background, and social milieu, if we are to understand the nature of his behavior and to determine which tools, approaches, and methods may be most effective in helping him.

Of course, many proponents of the ADD/ADHD paradigm will claim that they *do* in fact see the "ADD/ADHD child" through an interdisciplinary lens. The most effective approach for helping such a child, both in the diagnostic and treatment stages, according to their argument, is a team approach that involves not just the physician, but the psychologist, social worker, teacher or learning specialist, parent, and school administrator (Nathan, 1992; Whalen & Henker, 1991). In this team-based approach, each specialist provides input from her particular area of expertise in designing a coordinated treatment plan that embraces the child's total world both at school and in the home.

Such a team approach is vastly superior to the "teacher-refers-to-physician-who-prescribes-Ritalin" approach that characterizes so much of the *de facto* treatment of ADD/ADHD around the country. However, even this interdisciplinary perspective is limited when it places medical/biological factors at the center of the diagnosis (an inevitable outcome of the fact that ADD/ADHD has been defined from the outset as a biological disorder) (see Figure 2.1). Like a magnet, all other aspects of the child are drawn toward that medical-model label. ADD/ADHD experts will say that they are very sensitive to the issues of development, learning style, personality, gender, and social/cultural milieu (see, e.g., Barkley, 1990). These experts, however, are sensitive to these factors *only as they impinge on the medical diagnosis*. Here are some examples:

* *Developmental concerns* may be addressed in the ADD/ADHD world, but only insofar as a specific developmental stage (e.g., adolescence) may exacerbate the symptoms of ADHD or affect compliance in the taking of medications (see Robin, 1990).
* *Family systems approaches* may be used, but primarily as they enable the parents to learn new ways of effectively dealing with the child's ADD/ADHD-related problems, master effective child-management strategies, and receive support for stress caused by the ADD/ADHD (Barkley, 1990).
* *Learning* may be assessed, but only to determine if there are comorbid learning disabilities to go along with the ADD or ADHD (see Barkley, 1990, pp. 75–77).

In each case, instead of considering the possibility that human development issues, family systems, or learning styles may account for some or all of the problem behavior, these factors function very much like satellites orbiting around a planet, or center of gravity, which is the medical-model "ADD/ADHD" diagnosis itself (see Figure 2.1).

Figure 2.1 illustrates the interaction of perspectives in the traditional ADD/ADHD view (see Barkley, 1990, p. 210). All roads essentially lead to the biological underpinnings of the disorder. As Chapter 1 points out, the medical basis for ADD/ADHD is the foundation upon which "experts" base all other aspects of the disorder.

Figure 2.1—Traditional ADD/ADHD Paradigm

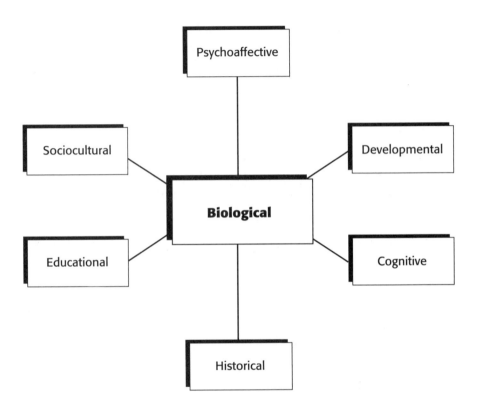

Even though outwardly it may appear as if people are discussing all aspects of the child's world during a meeting to assess a child's eligibility for the label of ADD/ADHD, or to discuss the possibilities for treatment, the biological paradigm all too often serves as the bottom line.

I'd like to suggest an approach that appears on the surface to be similar to the interdisciplinary approach described here, but that is fundamentally different in the way it approaches any discussion of a child who displays behavior described as hyperactive, distractible, or impulsive. Essentially, I'm proposing that we take the biological paradigm out from center stage, and replace it with the real focus of this entire inquiry, which is the whole child. When I say the "whole" child, I mean the child in all of his or her depth, breadth, richness, complexity, and uniqueness. I'm talking about the child who is beyond all labels, who defies pinning down onto any diagnostic map, who is always going to represent something of a mystery to us, given the ultimate mystery of life itself. Yet, I'm also speaking of a child whose wholeness we can begin to fathom, whose mystery we can begin to plumb, by availing ourselves of those special tools of understanding that are represented by the various perspectives or paradigms we have been discussing in the course of this book.

Each perspective—cognitive, educational, developmental, and so forth—provides a part of the truth with respect to the whole child. The difficulty comes when someone who has encountered one aspect of the whole child claims that he has discovered the "truth" of that child (e.g., the child suffers from ADD/ADHD, or has a "learning disability"). To guard against these limited views of the child, we need to make sure that we approach the child with awe and reverence, respecting the miracle of life and vitality that each child represents. As such, then, what belongs at the center is not any particular paradigm or narrowing point of view, but rather the wide horizon of the child's wholeness—her possibilities as well as her actualities, her strengths as well as her weaknesses, her individuality as well as her relation to the social matrix around her, her inner qualities as well as her external behavior, her known, as well as her unknown, and unknowable aspects (see Figure 2.2).

Note that the biological paradigm does not disappear from this holistic schematic. It rather ceases to be the central directing force, and assumes the role of another aspect of the child's whole world. Of course, for each unique child that exists at the center of this diagram,

Figure 2.2—A Holistic Schematic

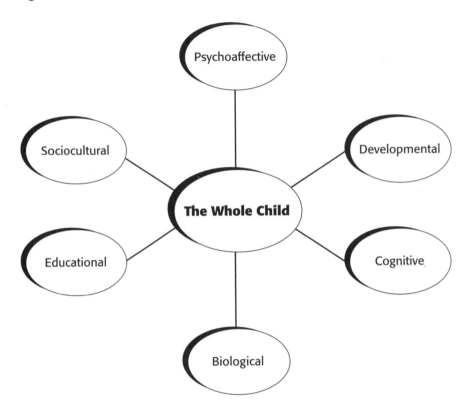

the importance of different paradigms may vary considerably. For a child who has suffered brain-damaging anoxia at birth, lead poisoning in infancy, a serious illness affecting the brain (such as encephalitis) in early childhood, or other clearly identifiable neurological insults, the biological paradigm may assume primary importance in the total picture of that child's behavior and attention span. For another child, however, it may be the cognitive paradigm that takes center stage (e.g., with a highly creative child), or the educational paradigm (e.g., for a strongly bodily-kinesthetic/spatial learner), or the developmental paradigm (e.g., for a "late bloomer"). Ultimately, of course, each paradigm will serve its part in providing helpful information about who the child is, and what can help him succeed in school and in the home. Each paradigm creates the possibility of new questions being asked about the child that can give rise to the broadest possible picture being taken about what he is capable of, and what he can really achieve in life.

Figure 2.3 suggests a few questions that a holistic perspective on attention and behavior problems might raise, most of which don't get asked in the ADD/ADHD paradigm. Also included are suggestions of who might be in the best position to ask such questions, what types of assessments might be used to gather information, and what sorts of interventions might be appropriate.

Note that I have framed the questions in this figure in a positive way, so that we might construct a picture of who this child *is* and what she *has*, not what she lacks. As mentioned earlier in this book, one of the most unfortunate features of the ADD/ADHD paradigm is that it represents a *deficit* paradigm where the focus is on discovering either that the child is *attention-deficit disordered*, or that he *isn't* ADD/ADHD. In the ADD/ADHD paradigm, the negatives hold the high cards:

- When educators and others explore educational issues, people taking the ADD/ADHD perspective look at these issues primarily in terms of what is going wrong (e.g., low grades, poor scores on tests, possibilities of learning disabilities).

- In the cognitive domain, these same people seem to have no real interest in exploring the nature of the child's mind *in its own right*, but rather against the framework of whether there are specific deficits of attention and memory.

- In the developmental domain, people tend to identify the possibilities of "immaturity," without considering that the child may have

Figure 2.3—Questions and Answers from Various Perspectives

Paradigm or Perspective	Key Question	Key Experts	Examples of Potential Assessments	Examples of Potential Interventions
Sociocultural	How much of the child's attention and behavior difficulties results from cultural differences?	Culturally sensitive social worker, psychologist, teacher	Home visits; classroom observations	Provision of culturally sensitive curriculum; celebration of cultural diversity
Psychoaffective	How much of the child's attention and behavior difficulties results from emotional trauma, anxiety/depression, or temperamental differences?	Clinical psychologist; psychiatrist; licensed counselor	Assessments for depression, anxiety; temperament assessments	Psychotherapy; family therapy; provision of emotionally supportive classroom environment
Developmental	How much of the child's attention and behavior difficulties results from a different pace of development?	Developmental pediatrician; child development specialist	Child development indexes; observation in natural settings	Provision of developmentally appropriate curriculum; readjustment of behavioral expectations
Cognitive	How much of the child's attention and behavior difficulties results from creative behavior or other positive cognitive differences?	Gifted and talented specialist; cognitive psychologist	Creativity instruments; cognitive style assessments	Use of expressive arts, creative curriculum, gifted and talented curriculum, and other creative approaches
Biological	How much of the child's attention and behavior difficulties results from biological problems or neurobiological differences?	Family physician; medical specialist (e.g., neurologist, psychiatrist)	Medical examination; specialized medical tests	Medications (e.g., Ritalin); treatment for underlying physical problems
Educational	How much of the child's attention and behavior difficulties results from learning differences?	Learning specialist; classroom teacher	Learning style inventories; multiple intelligences assessments, authentic assessments, portfolios of the child's work	Teaching strategies tailored to the child's individual learning style/multiple intelligences

a different developmental pace or express neotenic characteristics of neoteny (see p. 41).

The literature on the use of labels like ADHD and LD suggests that children can be negatively stigmatized by them (Harris, Milich, Corbitt, Hoover, & Brady, 1992; Rosenthal, 1978; Rosenthal & Jacobson, 1968; Sutherland & Algozzine, 1979). This use of labeling is particular devastating with children identified as ADD/ADHD who, the literature suggests, already suffer from poor self-esteem, learned helplessness, and an external locus of control (Linn & Hodge, 1982; Milich & Okazaki, 1991).

In this holistic approach to ADD/ADHD, I've tried to ask questions that keep us out of the negatives, in such a way that we can view the child as a complete human being, possessing strengths and limitations—but, most important, in such a way that we are able to see the child, ultimately as a whole human being.

3

STRATEGIES TO EMPOWER, NOT CONTROL, KIDS LABELED ADD/ADHD

Once we begin to work with a holistic approach to the ADD/ ADHD issue, we can envision many more possibilities for strategies to help kids who have attention and behavior difficulties. As it is, most ADD/ADHD advocates tend to have a conservative attitude toward the range of strategies that might help an individual child. Recent books on the subject for teachers and parents have stressed the necessity of being on guard against "unproven treatments for ADD/ ADHD" (e.g., Ingersoll & Goldstein, 1993). Some of this advice is well founded, because there are commercial companies out there claiming that their products (e.g., an herb, a potion, a set of lights and sounds, a kit, or some other merchandise designed to make the manufacturer rich) will "cure" or dramatically improve the behavior of people with ADD/ADHD.

The problem is, however, that most books on ADD/ADHD tend to approve only a very few "treatments" (usually, medication, cognitive-behavioral therapy, parent training, and a few educational accommodations), while regarding anything else as "unscientific." Ingersoll and Goldstein (1993), for example, insist that new techniques or substances pass through the most rigorous of experimental designs, the double-blind placebo controlled study, to qualify as a valid treatment (the sort of study that is used to validate the effectiveness of Ritalin, for example, or other psychoactive medications). This criterion works very well for medications, but not necessarily for other kinds of interventions.

Many important advances in the fields of medicine, psychology, psychiatry, and education have evolved through alternative research methodologies. Examples include psychoanalysis (individual case studies), the hazards of smoking (longitudinal studies), and cooperative learning (use of comparison groups). Because the ADD/ADHD paradigm relies so heavily on biological principles, this demand for rigid criteria that are appropriate to the medical field is perfectly understandable, but unfortunately misapplied. Once we break out of the biological paradigm and adopt a more holistic approach to the ADD/ADHD issue, we can entertain a far wider range of techniques, methods, tools, and research methodologies.

In this chapter, I present a sampling of such practical ideas for consideration in helping kids with attention and behavior difficulties. These ideas include educational, cognitive, physical, affective, biological, ecological, and behavioral strategies. Please note that I am not touting these strategies as "treatments for ADD/ADHD." In moving toward a holistic approach to the issue, I am concerned not with treating a disorder, but rather with helping a child.

In the previous chapter, I suggested that each child who displays behavior and attention difficulties possesses a unique constellation of factors that defines his individual world. Thus, we as educators must offer techniques, strategies, and tools that are diverse enough to meet the needs of many different kinds of children, and not just treat a hypothetical "ADHD" child.

Educational Strategies

The ADD/ADHD field has shown a particular lack of imagination in terms of providing educational strategies to help kids with attention and behavior difficulties. This is curious, inasmuch as so-called "ADD/ADHD children" often receive their labels through behavior that originates in school settings. One would think that researchers would have developed a wide range of creative techniques to help these students learn, attend, and behave more effectively in the classroom.

As it is, educational guidelines in the ADD/ADHD field tend to be stale and even at times clueless. A "fact sheet" put out for educators by CH.A.D.D., the key advocacy group for ADD/ADHD in the United States, includes this imperative: "Use the student's first name before calling on him or her" (CH.A.D.D., 1994). I can only wonder, What was the teacher doing before this? Other suggestions are simply bland or obvious: "Display classroom rules," "Allow more time to complete assignments or tests," "Make eye contact with the student before calling on him or her or giving instructions."

Many other books and guides for teachers in the field tend to focus a great deal of their attention on making the "ADD/ADHD child" adjust to a traditional classroom setting (e.g., organizing paperwork, remembering workbook assignments, listening to the teacher's lectures). Tips include using smiley stickers as rewards, giving praise, breaking up tasks into smaller bits, seating the child near the teacher's desk, and using organizational tools like dividers for notebooks and Post-Its® for reminders (Braswell, Bloomquist, & Pederson, 1991; Parker, 1992).

One wonderful exception to this trend is the work of Sydney Zentall at Purdue University. She and her colleagues have emphasized providing a stimulating learning environment. Her underlying premise is that many children who are identified as ADD or ADHD are understimulated, and require higher doses of stimulation than the "average" person—this being the reason why Ritalin—a stimulant—

may be so effective in calming behavior and focusing attention (Zentall, 1975; Zentall & Zentall, 1983). Zentall has engaged in numerous studies involving the use of color, sound, and other stimulus enhancers, which indicate that the selective and appropriate use of certain types of stimulation in the classroom is especially effective in helping kids with this label focus better on their learning (Zentall, 1993a and b; Zentall & Kruczek, 1988; Zentall & Zentall, 1976). Zentall's work is one of the few true beacons of light in an otherwise uninspiring field of ADD/ADHD educational researchers (for another creative approach, see Reif, 1993).

What is so dispiriting about the relative lack of development of innovative educational strategies in the ADD/ADHD field is that the wider field of education has been engaged in a veritable Renaissance of new ideas over the past 20 years. Educational innovations, such as learning styles, brain-based learning, cooperative learning, and authentic assessment, have revolutionized the way we view learning and teaching. Why has the ADD/ADHD field lagged so far behind? A holistic approach to ADD/ADHD seeks to incorporate many of these innovations into work with kids identified as ADD/ADHD, including multiple intelligences, incidental learning, and educational technology.

Multiple Intelligences

Howard Gardner's (1983, 1993) theory of multiple intelligences (MI) provides a rich framework for designing learning experiences that mesh with the special "proclivities" (intelligence areas of greatest interest or competence) of kids labeled ADD/ADHD. The eight intelligences in MI theory—linguistic, logical-mathematical, spatial, bodily-kinesthetic, musical, interpersonal, intrapersonal, and naturalist—provide a pedagogical palette that the teacher can draw from in creating just the right activity or strategy to suit a particular student. The child whose attention flags and behavior flares when learning about the Civil War through books and lectures may become absorbed in the material if it is presented through images, music, or role-play. The student who forgets to do her book report or math problems as homework may get absorbed in a learning project that involves interviewing a grandparent for social studies (interpersonal), taking pictures of animals in the neighborhood for an ecology unit (spatial-naturalist), or writing a song on an electronic keyboard about a character in a short story (musical).

Over the past few years, teachers and researchers have developed a wide range of books, manuals, videotapes, and other educational resources that offer a rich collection of ideas, strategies, and activities for virtually every area of the curriculum using multiple intelligences (see, e.g., Armstrong, 1994; Campbell, Campbell, & Dickinson, 1996; Haggerty, 1995; Lazear, 1991). Teachers can adapt many of these materials for one-to-one work with a student.

Also, several sources are available for exploring new ways to assess kids using MI principles (Gardner, 1993; Krechevsky, 1991; Lazear, 1994; Scrip, 1990). Thus, for the child who doesn't pay attention during tests, developing authentic assessment instruments based on multiple intelligences can provide a context within which teachers can better engage that student's attention. The child whose mind wanders during a paper-and-pencil item about the traits of a character in a story may come to life when the teacher asks him to pantomime the role as a way of showing his knowledge of character development.

MI works quite well as a means to develop specific *attention-grabbing* techniques. For the student who doesn't line up for lunch after hearing the teacher's linguistic instructions ("O.K. kids, it's time to line up!"), seeing a blown-up photo or slide of the class all lined up for lunch (taken by the teacher on a previous occasion) may trigger the spatial areas of the brain to respond by immediately lining up.

Zentall (1993b) reported using music to engage a girl labeled ADD to remember her homework assignments. The teacher made a cassette recording of her homework instructions, followed by her favorite musical selections, and then more homework instructions. The girl would rush home every day to listen to her tape, and her ability to remember homework assignments rose dramatically. Some teachers have developed specific bodily-kinesthetic "cues" with students to signal certain classroom instructions (e.g., rubbing the tummy means it's time for lunch, lowering both outstretched hands means "Bring down the energy level a notch or two," a finger pointed to the temple means "Remember to take your assignment home").

Finally, perhaps the most powerful—and exciting—application of MI theory involves teaching it to students. Many teachers find it very easy to teach (it may help to use simpler terms, such as *word smart, number smart, picture smart, music smart, body smart, people smart, self smart*, and *nature smart*). It's important to emphasize that everyone has *all eight* kinds of smart. For the student who may feel disheartened by hearing everyone talk about him as a "deficit disordered" learner, MI theory provides a new—and positive—vocabulary to describe how he learns best, and what he may need in a particular learning situation to respond in a positive way (see Armstrong, 1994; Lazear, 1993).

Incidental Learning

Incidental learning is the way that all of us learned during the first few years of life. It refers to nondirected learning; the kind of learning that takes place in the course of ordinary life; the knowledge that we acquire by simply absorbing it from the environment in incidental ways. The manner in which youngsters learn to talk is a good illustration of this kind of learning. Parents do not sit down and teach their infants words one-at-a-time (or at least, they shouldn't!). Rather, the youngster learns by listening to others speak, imitating them, receiving spontaneous feedback from parents and others, and practicing the sounds she hears. In the same way, so many other things that we've learned, from riding a bike to getting along with our boss, have been acquired through incidental learning.

Most teachers, unfortunately, do not value incidental learning. What's important in most classrooms is that students direct their attention to very specific stimuli: the teacher's voice, test item number 24, the math problems on page 97, the assignment on the blackboard. These are precisely the sorts of requirements that many kids labeled ADD/ADHD have the hardest time with in the classroom. They either cannot or will not pay attention to such central-task stimuli unless prodded to do so with behavior modification reinforcements or other inducements (including medication).

Some research suggests, however, that many of these kids may in fact possess *superior* incidental attention. In other words, they pay most attention to things that they're not supposed to be paying attention to! While the teacher is talking, they're listening to what Frank is telling Sam in the back of the classroom. They're reading the graffiti on the blackboard that the teacher didn't even notice. They hear footsteps in the hall, or a fire-engine siren in the distance.

The biggest mistake that many teachers make with this kind of incidental attention is ignoring it or trying to force it back to central-task attention. Teachers who value incidental learning find ways to bring the two types of attention together. For example, a teacher may be reading a story about a character named Barney, who is lost in the woods. Suddenly, a fire engine goes by the school in real life. Instead of fighting it ("Class! Let's have your attention! Joseph! That's a point off!"), the sensitive teacher might respond, "And that's the sound of the rescue trucks coming to help poor Barney!" Immediately, the "incidental" stimulus becomes the central one, and the child whose attention has "wandered" suddenly finds himself back in the middle of the story!

An entire system of education has developed in the past 25 years around this notion of incidental learning. Originally developed by a Bulgarian psychiatrist, Georgi Lozanov, *suggestopedia*, "super-learning" or "accelerative learning" as it is usually called in the United States, has developed a wide range of learning activities that make use of students' "incidental attention" in achieving academic gains (Lozanov, 1978; Rose, C., 1989; Schuster & Gritton, 1986). Here are some examples:

• Teachers may introduce vocabulary or spelling words to a class by putting decorative posters on the walls the week before they are officially introduced. As the eyes of students wander around the classroom that week, they often focus on the posters and the spelling words (remember, they're not *supposed* to be paying attention to the words that week!). As a result, they are often more successful in learning them during the "official" week they're presented.

• Students listen to material recited by the teacher in a rhythmic way while listening to background music. The students are instructed "not to listen to the teacher's voice but just to relax and enjoy the music." Research studies suggest that this approach to learning can be very powerful in acquiring certain kinds of knowledge, such as a foreign language (Druckman & Swets, 1988).

• Drama is also used as a part of accelerative learning. A teacher may present a lesson as a puppet show or dramatically dress up in a costume to illustrate a point about a subject (this reminds me of Jaime Escalante dressed up in an apron with an apple and cleaver to illustrate fractions to his math class in the movie *Stand and Deliver*).

These are the sorts of activities that students will remember long after they've left school. The memories last because the actions of the teacher "riveted" the students' attention. In a field dedicated to helping kids with attention problems, it's truly amazing to me that so little has been printed in the ADD/ADHD literature about how teachers can vividly capture students' attention.

Quite apart from the fact that incidental learning can be used to teach material directly relevant to the teacher's objectives, sometimes students' "off-task" behavior can be quite educational. In one study, Dyson (1987) noted that children's off-task verbal behavior helped them develop intellectual skills. In other studies, children identified as ADHD showed more creative, spontaneous talk than so-called normals (Zentall, 1988), and often showed in their nonsanctioned "private speech" the capacity to organize thinking that was actually quite task-relevant (Berk & Landau, 1993). Most child development theorists emphasize that children's free unstructured play—which could be called "self-directed, off-task behavior"—contributes to a child's intellectual, social, and emotional welfare and even to humanity's adaptation to changing environments (Mann, D., 1996; Sutton-Smith, 1998).

During my five years of teaching kids with behavior and attention difficulties, I always had a time during the day—usually 20–30 minutes—of "choice time." During this time, students were free to engage in "unstructured off-task behavior" of their own choosing (including painting, reading, drama, carpentry, typing, and listening to music). For many kids, this time was the best part of their day.

It remains for educators to see the value in children's "off-task" or "incidental" learning, and make use of it to help kids be successful in school and life—especially those kids labeled ADD/ADHD who may do much of their learning in this way.

Educational Technology

As I stated in Chapter 2, many children labeled ADD/ADHD are products of our "short-attention-span" society, moulded as they have been by quickly shifting images from television, video games, and computer software. In Chapter 2, I emphasized the negative aspects of this contemporary phenomenon, how media moguls have shaped the attention spans of children (and adults), creating greater and greater demands for higher and higher levels of stimulation. I need to point out, however, that despite the many problems of the high-speed media phenomenon, it is here to stay. Like it or not, the shifting images and sounds are likely to be with us for the long term, and to become even faster and more jarring for educators who are accustomed to training children to process information in linear, one-step-a-time *knowledge units.*

Given the likelihood, then, of increased levels of high speed stimuli in the future, we should take advantage of this phenomenon—we need to explore the potential value of high-speech technology in helping kids labeled ADD/ADHD learn more effectively. In fact, it may be that kids with attentional and behavioral difficulties may be particularly well-suited to such technologies, given their propensity for high stimulation (Zentall, 1993a; Zentall & Zentall, 1976).

One of the biggest developments in computer technology over the past 10 years has been the advance of "*hyper*text" in software programs and in the vast linkage system of the Internet. The similarity in terms between "*hyper*text" and "*hyper*active child" cannot have escaped notice by at least a few educators. It appears as if this new nonlinear way of accessing information—through links that "click" to links that "click" to further links along a network of vast possibilities—mimics to at least some degree the workings of the minds of many kids with attentional or behavioral difficulties.

The ADD/ADHD literature has frequent references to this kind of nonlinear mind (Moss, 1990, p. 59). The problem is that this facility of mind is regarded in the deficit-based ADD/ADHD paradigm as a negative quality: *distractibility*. It is, in fact, one of the primary symptoms of ADD/ADHD. Regarded in a more positive way, however, this same quality can be considered as divergent, associative, or creative, and perfectly well-suited to the requirements of "surfing the net." In fact, in such a cyber-environment, the person who processes information best in the old-fashioned linear way prized by schools for centuries may be at a distinct disadvantage. The popular literature is full of examples of people who have risen to prominence in the computer industry over the past 20 years who did not thrive well in traditional school environments and who are bringing an entirely new ethos to the world of business and the broader culture (see, e.g., Rose, F., 1987). It remains for the educational world to explore in detail the relationship of this new divergent way of processing information with the associative minds of kids labeled ADD/ADHD.

In fact, the research suggests that computer technology is a highly effective approach for kids identified as ADD/ADHD (Bender & Bender, 1996; Ford, Poe, & Cox, 1993; Millman, 1984). The advantages of the computer for kids with attentional and behavioral difficulties include the following:

- High-speed, instant feedback
- Ability to self-control stimuli
- Bright colors and sounds
- Interactive aspects

Of course, we can certainly bore children with poor computer software programs—for example, electronic versions of the worksheets, tests, workbooks, lectures, and verbal directions that bored them before. But designers of innovative programs have found ways of avoiding these pedagogical pitfalls and stimulating high levels of interest, attention, and performance with all kids.

In addition to computer software and the Internet, the educationally sound use of television, film, and other educational technologies may be particularly well suited to kids with short attention spans. Some research, indeed, points to the ability of kids labeled ADD to sustain normal attention levels while watching television (Landau, Lorch, & Milich, 1992). Other researchers have underlined the commonsense suggestion that parents and teachers should limit television, video games, and computer time with kids labeled ADHD—and should make sure they avoid all violent programming (Heusmann & Eron, 1986). But the judicious use of high-stimulation technology can provide an important educational resource to help these students acquire information in a way that is in synch with their hyper-minds.

Cognitive Strategies

As noted in Chapter 1 of this book, the term "attention-deficit disorder" is a *cognitive* construct. Thus the primary concern of those in the ADD/ADHD field ought to be how to better understand the ways in which children with this label actually think. Because the construct has developed within the context of a deficit or disease-based paradigm, however, research has actually tended to focus much more on how children identified as ADD/ADHD really *can't* think as well as "normal" kids (Hamlett, Pellegrini, & Conners, 1987; Penington, Groisser, & Welsh, 1993). As a result, what cognitive strategies that ADD/ADHD researchers and practitioners have developed have focused on getting these kids to think more like normal people.

Studies on the efficacy of cognitive approaches have produced mixed results in whether one can train the minds of children labeled ADD/ADHD to attend, remember, focus, or "think" more effectively (Abikoff, 1985; Fehlings, Roberts, Humphries, & Dawes, 1991). One reason for the mixed results may be that researchers are artificially imposing specific cognitive procedures on kids labeled ADD/ADHD without seeking to discover how these children *actually think*. We need research on the actual subjective experience going on inside of the minds of children with attentional and behavioral difficulties. Do these kids think in words, numbers, pictures, music, physical sensations, or in other ways? With the advent of new models of thinking and learning we now have more ways in which to contextualize the different ways of thinking in kids labeled ADD/ADHD (Gallas, 1994; Houston, 1982; Samples, 1976; Schwartz, 1992; Taylor, 1991).

Strategies like self-talk, visualization, and biofeedback may tap the natural cognitive assets that kids labeled ADD/ADHD have to help them succeed in and outside of the classroom.

Self-Talk

The use of words to help direct the mind toward specific goals is one of the central features of verbal activity in human beings. Young children organize much of their thinking through private speech, or the process of talking to themselves or to no one in particular (Vygotsky, 1986). Gradually as we develop, this stream of words becomes internalized as *inner speech*. The parallel chatter of youngsters at play is replaced by the "silent mind chatter" of adults at work.

The ADD/ADHD field has directed much of its attention in cognitive therapy to approaches that seek to train kids identified as ADD/ADHD to use "self-talk" strategies. Recent research suggests, however, that many kids with attentional and behavioral difficulties *may already possess* the ability to use task-relevant self-talk in the classroom, and that cognitive training programs are simply teaching them something they already know how to do (Berk & Landau, 1993). Berk and Landau suggest that teachers arrange classroom environments to allow such children to use their already naturally occurring private speech during work periods in such a way that they are not disturbing others.

Berk and Potts (1991) have pointed out that some children labeled ADD/ADHD may continue to use private speech after others in the classroom have internalized their self-talk as silent mind chatter. In such environments, this self-talk may stick out and be regarded as "off-task" or "disruptive" behavior (and even used to affirm the diagnosis of ADD/ADHD). By understanding that these kids may need to use their natural self-talk capabilities while working to help them think more effectively, teachers may come to see these types of behavior as a positive educational tool, not as a disruptive behavior.

Visualization

Children with attentional and behavioral difficulties may process information more readily through posterior, spatial areas of the brain than through anterior, linguistic areas (Mulligan, 1996; Sunshine et al., 1997). In such cases, visualization rather than self-talk may be the preferred way of organizing thinking. These kids may be the daydreamers in class—perhaps those who are not as outwardly active or talkative, but rather inwardly drawn to their imaginative faculties, and thus more likely to be diagnosed as ADD without hyperactivity: *distractible, forgetful, disorganized.*

The linguistic bias of our schools and culture is so strong that there is no research base to speak of on the visualization capabilities of children labeled ADD/ADHD. We need to have studies that look into the minds of these kids and attempt to discover the nature of the images that form the basis of their daydreams, fantasies, and imaginations while they sit staring off into space in the classroom.

Of special interest would be the extent to which those images are connected in some way with the curriculum. It has been noted by ADD/ADHD experts (e.g. Moss, 1990) that kids with attentional difficulties often have associative minds that may be triggered by a task-relevant event in the classroom but then spin off from that stimulus into associations that are considered offtask. I believe we should study the patterns of these thoughts—especially those that are based on images—to determine how they might be used in the service of the curriculum.

Some educational researchers have investigated the use of visualization, guided imagery, imagination, and similar tools to help students learn content more effectively (Allender, 1991; Murdock, 1989). Educators should learn how to use these resources to help students labeled ADD/ADHD with high visualization or imagination skills. For example, a teacher might lead a student on an imaginative journey through the circulatory system to help her master certain anatomical concepts. Or a child might be taught how to visualize the steps of a math problem, the plot of a story, the spelling of a word, a scene from history, a strategy for coping with anger, or a way of picturing himself as a successful learner.

Researchers have found some evidence that these approaches may be successful with kids who have behavior and attention difficulties (Murdock, 1989; Schneidler, 1973). And just as spontaneous self-talk may be a natural ability in some kids labeled ADD/ADHD to help them to think and work more effectively, we ought to explore whether something similar might be true with respect to spontaneous image production. In such cases, we may want to encourage the active imagination of certain students while they study.

Focusing Techniques

For thousands of years, cultures in every part of the world have developed techniques and systems of training attention: tai-chi, yoga, meditation, introspection, visionary quests, rites of passage, reflection, reverie, and more (Dang, 1994; Goleman, 1996; Iyengar, 1995). It strikes me as curious that in a field dedicated to helping children who struggle with their attention, there is scarcely a mention in the ADD/ADHD literature of any of these attention-training methods. Yet other educational books and articles include references to the use of various techniques to help kids labeled ADD/ADHD train their ability to focus on a stimulus. In one study, adapted from an approach used by Harvard physician Herbert Benson (Benson & Klipper, 1990), kids labeled ADD/ADHD who were asked to focus on a sound for a few minutes each day, experienced less distractibility and impulsivity, and greater ability to attend (Kratter & Hogan, 1982).

In other examples, researchers trained kids to focus on images. Oaklander (1978) used a "roaming meditation" as a part of her work with children who could not hold their focus on a single object for more than a second or two (pp. 226–227). She asked a child to report on what he was looking at "right now"; and as his attention shifted, she asked him again, "What do you see now?" and continued this process until his ability to attend to one thing gradually increased.

Biofeedback

A more recent tool for training attention uses technology. Biofeedback seeks to help people identified as ADD/ADHD regulate their own electrical activity within the brain. The human brain generates very small electrical currents that can be measured on an electroencelphalogram (EEG). These currents vary in amplitude, depending on the state of mind of the person who is hooked up to an EEG machine.

The results depict varying types of brain waves, as follows:

• For an adult in a quiet, resting state, much of the EEG record will consist of *alpha waves* repeating themselves at the back of the head at about 10 hertz (a hertz is an international unit of frequency equal to one cycle per second).

• More focused states of alertness produce a more rapid rhythm in the central and frontal portions of the brain (18–25 hertz) and are referred to as *beta waves*.

• Slow rhythmic waves occurring at frequencies of 4–7 hertz are called *theta waves* and are considered normal activity in infants and young children, but tend to decrease during the elementary school years. Theta waves tend to be associated with daydreaming, creativity, hypnogogic imagery, and a wide focus of attention.

Some research suggests that certain children with attentional and behavioral difficulties produce more theta (wide focus) and less beta (narrow focus) than do comparison groups (Lubar & Lubar, 1984). These results are consistent with some of our observations regarding the imagination, creativity, and wide focus of many kids identified as ADD/ADHD. Biofeedback training may help these kids generate less theta and more beta, thus improving their ability to focus and concentrate on task-specific stimuli.

Biofeedback training typically consists of several sessions in which a child who is hooked up to an EEG device is invited to cause stimuli on a computer screen to respond in a certain way (e.g., keep a boat afloat, make a yellow ball stay within two green squares). He is instructed to do whatever he needs to do, using only his mind, to control the objects. Although this field is controversial—training background for professionals using biofeedback varies tremendously and claims for "ADD cures" are unfounded—some types of biofeedback training may be helpful for certain kids with the ADD/ADHD label (see Lee, 1991).

Physical Strategies

The most visible signs of children who have been labeled ADD/ADHD (especially ADHD) involve physical movement: fidgeting, squirming, and running around when required to be seated or be quiet. Why not focus on the physicality of these children, with the intention of developing strategies to help them be more successful in the classroom? The ADD/ADHD paradigm, generally speaking, sees this physicality as a problem. The emphasis in "treatment" is on seeking ways of subduing "excess" movement in these kids so that they can sit still long enough to focus on the material at hand.

One of the most frequently cited phrases in the ADD/ADHD treatment literature relates to the need to help these kids: "STOP, LOOK, and LISTEN!" Such a perspective, however, usually requires external control of the child, including medication and behavior modification, to be successful. Moreover, it is based on a traditional model of education that sees optimum learning taking place under conditions where children are seated quietly at their desks, rather than while learning in more dynamic ways.

A holistic approach, on the other hand, validates the child *as he is*, seeking to understand the potential value of his high levels of physical energy, and searching for ways to make that physicality a positive asset in the classroom. As pointed out earlier in this book, many kids labeled ADHD may, in fact, be highly developed bodily-kinesthetic learners—kids who learn best by moving, touching, building, dramatizing, and experiencing the material of the curriculum in other physical ways. As such, educational approaches based on role play, hands-on learning, and other kinds of dynamic learning may be more appropriate ways of helping ADHD-labeled kids be more effective in the classroom. It might be far better for educators to develop innovative methods to help these kids: "GO, LOOK, and LISTEN!" In this section, I suggest several strategies that are based on this positive perspective, such as allowing *appropriate* movement, providing hands-on instruction, and promoting a strong physical education program.

Allow Appropriate Movement

Once, after a lecture I gave on the ADD/ADHD issue, a teacher came up to me and said: "You know, I always give a kid like that two desks: one desk on this side of the room, and another on the opposite end. That way, if he gets out of his desk, he's always moving toward his other desk!" Whether or not you agree with this particular strategy, what makes it interesting is that the teacher has attempted to take behavior that is usually disruptive (getting out of his desk frequently) and turn it into appropriate behavior (moving toward his "other desk").

This general philosophy has guided the strategies of many good teachers over the years to help "high movers" in the classroom be successful. Another teacher told me about a student who was constantly fidgeting, out of his desk, and failing in reading class. One day, the teacher had forgotten to water the plants and asked this student to go to the back of the room and do the watering. While he did this, she gave the phonics lesson for the day. Later on, when the class was tested on the material, it turned out that this was the first time he got 100 percent correct on the test! She realized that he was a student who needed to move while learning, and so she started designing other chores and activities he could do during lectures.

In the ADD/ADHD world, teachers are instructed to seat a child labeled ADD/ADHD at the front of the class, near the teacher so she can keep an eye on him (CH.A.D.D., 1994). The problem with this strategy is that the student can twist and turn and fall out of his chair to the amusement of all the students in the class. Many teachers I've talked with have been more successful in letting such students sit at the back of the classroom with the understanding that if they need to get up and stretch or move around (where they can't be directly seen by most students), they can do so as long as they don't disturb anyone. In one case, a teacher enlisted the help of a parent volunteer to create a lectern at the *back* of the classroom for a child identified as hyperactive, where he could study sitting down or standing up (Markowitz, 1986). They installed a sewing machine treadle at the bottom so he could keep his feet in motion, and lined the inside of the lectern with felt so that he could get tactile stimulation.

Other teachers have provided opportunities for kids to be physical while learning by using a "reading rocking chair," a minitrampoline, and a "math bathtub" (a freestanding bathtub that students are allowed to get into, but only to do math homework!). Some teachers even give kids little squeeze balls so that they can keep their hands busy while they are listening to the teacher or reading a book.

These suggestions are all based on helping to channel the physical activity of specific kids in the midst of an otherwise nonphysical classroom environment where most kids are sitting quietly in their desks. The limitation of these strategies is that they do not directly relate to the curriculum. Far more powerful strategies for allowing appropriate movement in the classroom tie the activities directly into the teaching/learning process itself and involve *all* students, not just those with the ADD/ADHD label. Here are some ways of doing this:

• Learning spelling words by having kids jump up out of their seats on the vowels and sit down on the consonants.

- Mastering the multiplication tables by forming a conga line, moving around the classroom counting from 1 to 30 out loud, and on every multiple of 3 shaking their hips and legs.
- Acquiring historical knowledge by role playing a "typical" day in the life of a Puritan household in Massachusetts in the 1640s.
- Showing patterns of molecular bonding in chemistry class through a "swing your atom" square dance.
- Demonstrating an understanding of character development in a novel by having students pantomime the rise and fall of selected figures in literature.
- Understanding the impact of geographic terrain on the experiences of Lewis and Clark by having the class take a simulated "journey" across the classroom.

Moreover, kids with attentional and behavioral difficulties may benefit from *any* special project that requires students to function in cooperative groups, interview others, engage in labwork, build structures, play learning games, or move actively in other curriculum-related activities. Such projects provide important potential outlets for the physical energies of kids labeled ADHD (Griss, 1998; Hannaford, 1995; Patterson, 1997).

Teach Physical Relaxation Skills

Another way to help kids labeled ADHD cope with high levels of physical activity in school settings where they cannot always move as they'd like is to show them how to modulate their physical tensions through specific relaxation techniques using yoga, progressive relaxation, isometrics, breathing, and imagery (Stewart, 1993; Williams, 1996). Here are some examples:

- One of the simplest techniques is to teach a student how to alternatively flex and relax different muscles in his body to help discharge some of the muscular tension that he wants to express in more overt ways (this is called *progressive relaxation*). You can teach students a one-minute progressive relaxation procedure that they can do at their desks quietly without others in the classroom even noticing.

- Similarly, you can show students how to take a deep breath, hold it briefly, relax, then repeat the procedure a few more times, as needed. Such deep breathing can help some students discharge physical energy and also center their focus of attention when they feel fidgety or restless.

- Use visualization strategies involving kinesthetic imagery, such as letting students know that they can "physically move around in your mind" (e.g., "Do 40 push-ups in your imagination") instead of moving around the classroom. This can help students transform their physical energy into mental energy that can then be "acted out" internally with no disruption to the class.

Researchers have reported favorably on the use of many of these techniques with students described as "hyperactive," "ADHD," or "behavior problems" (Dunn, F. M., & Howell, 1986; Omizo, 1981; Richter, 1984).

Provide Opportunities for Hands-On Learning

Many years ago, children who had particularly strong needs to learn through physical involvement were described as "haptic" learners, from the Greek *haptos*, meaning "to lay a hold of" (Lowenfeld, 1987). These were kids who learned best by laying a hold of whatever was available in the learning environment.

Today, at least some kids who are actually haptic learners might be at risk of being labeled ADD/ADHD (Locher, 1995). If there are no meaningful hands-on materials available for learning, these children will nevertheless grab whatever is available—a neighbor's hair-do, an action toy brought from home, somebody else's pen—and many educators will then regard these kinds of behavior as *warning signs* of ADHD. One potential solution for these kids would be to create rich opportunities for hands-on learning so that they can "lay a hold" of materials that relate directly to success in the classroom. Here are a few suggestions:

• Use manipulatives to learn math concepts (e.g., Cuisenaire rods, Dienes blocks, UNIFIX cubes) (Davidson, 1996).
• Create battlefields (using miniature soldiers, game boards, and other materials) to illustrate major conflicts during the Revolutionary War.
• Employ hands-on lab materials to teach science concepts.
• Build dioramas that set the scenes for particular events in a short story or novel.
• Design building structures to learn about architecture.
• Make 3-D relief maps to show geographic features of the local region.
• Form letters out of clay to learn alphabet shapes.
• Invent and build special machines to illustrate cause and effect.

Just as teachers encourage students to write down or draw their ideas in class, there also should be opportunities for students to create hands-on models that represent their current thinking on a school-related topic. For example, if students are learning about the concept of the *national debt* in economics, teachers might give them balls of clay and ask them to create a 3-D representation of a potential solution to the national debt.

You can use many other hands-on materials as well for concept formation, including pipe cleaners, wire, blocks, collages, or even a simple piece of white paper that can be torn, crumpled, or formed in other ways to represent a "kinesthetic sculpture" of a concept. For example, students could create paper sculptures of the following vocabulary words: *bulbous*, *fragmentary*, and *elongated*. When kids labeled ADD/ADHD are allowed to use their hands to express what is in their minds, they may well be able to produce some very creative, unexpected results and display positive traits that were hidden under a landslide of negative behavior.

Promote a Strong Physical Education Program in the School

When the American Pediatric Association issued a position statement on the use of Ritalin a few years ago, they suggested that educators use a number of alternative strategies *before* physicians prescribed a trial of psychostimulants for an individual child. Among the alternatives listed was "a strong physical education program." (American Academy of Pediatrics, 1987).

Every good teacher knows that a run around the school two or three times is a natural prescription for a restless class or student. A strong physical education that builds in regular opportunities for physical release and other forms of physical culture, however, represents a far sounder approach to help students deal with their restless physical energies. Unfortunately, very few schools and school systems in the United States promote strong physical education programs; and many existing programs are limited to calisthenics and a few competitive games (Portner, 1993).

According to recent research (Seefeldt & Vogel, 1990; Virgilio & Berenson, 1988), a strong physical education program should involve a total approach to physical culture including some of the following:

- Individual and competitive sports.
- Fitness programs.
- Martial arts.
- Yoga.
- Creative movement and dance.

A small literature on the subject suggests that such programs can be helpful for kids labeled ADD/ADHD (Alexander, 1990; Coat, 1982; Putnam & Copans, 1998). As neuroscientist Jaak Panksepp (1996) writes:

> Clearly, the developing human brain and psyche were not designed to sit quietly in classrooms for hours on end. . . . Rather the brain was designed to frolic with other youngsters, especially out-of-doors (p. 3).

Panksepp suggests that the gradual disappearance of brain-friendly "rough-and-tumble play" in our culture may be correlated to the increased incidence of attention disorders in our classrooms. A strong physical education program in our schools can help provide some of the high physical stimulation that many kids labeled ADD/ADHD may require on a daily basis.

Affective Strategies

Although a few authorities working within the ADD/ADHD paradigm have written about the inner emotional worlds of kids labeled ADD/ADHD (Brooks, 1992, 1994; Heilveil & Clark, 1990), the literature as a whole is sadly lacking in a rich account of the personal emotions of these kids. Here are questions we need answers to:

- What are these kids feeling inside?
- What are they wishing for?

- What are they despairing of?
- Who and what do they despise?
- What fills them with passion and joy?
- How they do feel about themselves?
- How do they feel about school? About their friends? About their parents?

Whereas the ADD/ADHD field has focused its attention on external behavior, internal thinking processes, and biological causality, any attempt to understand the needs of kids identified as ADD/ADHD requires that we also have a sense of their inner emotional lives. We need this understanding to help them become successful in school and life.

In Chapter 2, we've examined research suggesting that some of these kids may be hyperactive, impulsive, or distractible because they experience severe emotional disturbance underneath the surface of these external kinds of behavior. Other kids with the label who display evidence of creative behavior may experience a rich inner emotional world that is perceived by authorities as "disruptive" or "ADHD" only because it is unconventional (Cramond, 1994; Reid, B. D., & McGuire, 1995)

Still other kids may experience deep feelings of unworthiness because of the effect of negative school, peer, or parenting experiences. In some cases, the response of educators to such deep-seated emotional upset should be to make a proper referral to a licensed mental-health professional. In other instances, the role of the educator should be to directly address the affective domain in school so that these emotions serve to enhance and not disrupt the classroom experience. Strategies like encouraging the expressive arts, holding a positive image, and using positive role models can help accomplish this objective.

Expressive Arts

One might regard the behaviors that make up a description of ADD/ADHD—hyperactivity, distractibility, and impulsivity—as "misdirected energy." The expressive arts provide an opportunity to reroute that energy in a positive direction. Researchers have suggested that many kids labeled ADD/ADHD do not display as much disruptive behavior when engaged in arts-oriented activities, such as painting, drama, dance, and play, as they do when involved in more traditional school-based tasks (Berlin, 1989; O'Neil, 1994; Smitheman-Brown & Church, 1996). These expressive arts provide ready-made channels within which the undirected energies of kids can be allowed to flow.

I noticed this myself when codirecting an arts resource room as a part of a summer special education program. Kids who would be disruptive in every other class would come to our arts room and immediately calm down as they got involved in mask-making, carpentry, model building, and other arts-related activities. Here are a few ideas for bringing the expressive arts into the worlds of kids identified as ADD/ADHD:

- Support a *strong arts-oriented program* at your school, with courses in dance, music, painting, drama, creative writing, sculpture, and other creative forms, and enroll kids labeled ADD/ADHD in arts courses that reflect their deepest interests.
- Provide a space in your classroom for *creative activity*, including puppets, paints, costumes for drama, and building materials. In my own classroom for kids with behavior problems, I used to have a "world-making" area, where kids could create miniature towns and cities using clay, figurines, toy vehicles, plastic trees, and other small play objects.

- Explore *opportunities outside of school* where a child identified as ADD/ADHD can take music, dance, or painting lessons; enroll in a children's theater company; or become involved in other ways with creative projects in the community.
- Build in opportunities for using the arts in *every part of the curriculum* (e.g., having kids do role-play in history lessons, draw pictures to illustrate math word problems, create raps and songs about characters in literature) (Margulies, 1991; Spolin, 1986; Wallace, 1992).

As educators begin to think about the symptoms of ADD/ADHD as untapped creative potential, we will see less of a tendency to pathologize kids with this label, and more of an opportunity to help these students realize their inner potential.

Holding a Positive Image

In this book, I've emphasized the problems in using negative labels to describe kids who are struggling with attention and behavior difficulties. This process of negative labeling adds insult to injury: It formalizes or institutionalizes the negative experiences of the student. If students are having difficulty with school, they certainly don't need to have a label hung around their necks that includes two negatives in it (attention *deficit disorder*). Rather, they should be surrounded by adults *who see the best in them.*

Consequently, one of the most important strategies in this book is for educators to work toward holding *positive* images about such students. Recently, several books have sought to reframe our perspectives on learners with behavior or attention problems within a positive context:

- The spirited child (Kurcinka, 1992).
- The active, alert child (Budd, 1993).

- The "hunter in a farmer's world" (Hartmann, 1997).
- The "right brained child in a left brained world" (Freed & Parsons, 1998).
- The child with "the Edison trait" (Palladino, 1997).

Here are some tips for holding a positive image for students labeled ADD/ADHD:

- Avoid using the ADD/ADHD labels as much as possible. If you must use the labels for administrative reasons or purposes of communication to others, however, I recommend you refer to "the child who has been labeled ADD" or "the student identified (or diagnosed) as having ADHD," rather than "the ADD child" or "the child with ADHD."

In the latter case, you acknowledge the child's ADD/ADHD status, but you do so in terms of the actual social fact of having been diagnosed or labeled (an event that actually occurred), rather than in terms of who the child *is*, or what the child *has* (suppositions that are questionable in the context of this book). This might seem like political correctness to some, but there is strong empirical support for the finding that what we tell other people about a student can affect that student's performance (Rosenthal, 1978; Rosenthal & Jacobson, 1968).

- Teach your ADD/ADHD-labeled students about models of learning that can help them understand themselves better. Rather than emphasizing the range of literature designed to help students understand their ADD/ADHD (e.g., Galvin, 1988; Gehret, 1991; Levine, 1992), I suggest instead, that teachers help students understand their *multiple intelligences* (Armstrong, 1994; Lazear, 1993), their *learning styles*, their *temperaments*, or other models of self-understanding. Certainly, if students receive the ADD/ADHD label, they deserve a frank and forthcoming explanation of what it means, but you should give this information in the context of a broader discussion about who the student really is and what he is capable of becoming.

• Make a detailed list of all the positive traits, types of positive behavior, talents, interests, intelligences, aptitudes, competencies, and abilities of each student you have who is labeled ADD/ADHD. Each time you feel overwhelmed by the negative behavior of this student, take out this list and study it. Visualize this student as a positive learner.

• Use a range of positive terms and descriptions when talking about a student labeled ADD/ADHD to others, including *spirited, passionate, creative, alive, exuberant,* and *imaginative.* You should not use these terms gratuitously or as a way of explaining away bad behavior. But they should serve as portals to more positive ways of thinking about these kids.

• Make sure you let students labeled ADD/ADHD know that you see them as positive learners. Contravene their negative descriptions of themselves with some of the positive terminologies we've described. Help them construct and hold an image of themselves as a highly competent individual.

Positive Role Models

I believe that students who have been labeled ADD/ADHD should be frequently reminded of famous people in history who struggled with similar difficulties in their lives. Such examples are not hard to find. Goertzel and Goertzel (1962) examined the lives of 400 eminent individuals in history and discovered that 300 of them disliked school! For example:

• Winston Churchill was thrown out of every school he ever attended as a child.

- Pope John XXIII was sent home from school with a note saying that he continually came to class unprepared, and he didn't even give the note to his parents!
- Beethoven was rude to his friends and highly disorganized in his home life.
- Louis Armstrong spent time in an institution for delinquent boys.
- Sarah Bernhardt was expelled from school three times.

I believe that educators should create mini-units of these "hyperactive heroes" and present this material to all students, but in particular to kids who have been labeled ADD/ADHD. I don't think it's appropriate to say, "These famous people had ADD/ADHD just like you." Rather, I feel that we should tell students: "You can make something of your life just like these great individuals—you have the same kind of passionate energy—if you learn to direct it—that these figures had to achieve greatness." Here are some ways to get this information across to students:

- Use photos, biographies, movies, and role play to make vivid the lives of these positive role models.
- Consider bringing into the classroom individuals from the community who have struggled with behavior problems in school and yet who have done well in their chosen fields.
- Explore careers in the world that require people with high levels of energy who like to move around, change activities frequently, and self-regulate their own work (e.g., self-employed businessperson, freelance writer, music or dance therapist, craftsperson, aerobic fitness instructor, public relations consultant, recreational worker, building contractor).

Ultimately, the objective should be to help students labeled ADD/ADHD think about their hyperactive role models and futures in a positive way and to come to this conclusion: "If they can do it, so can I!"

Interpersonal Strategies

The research literature within the ADD/ADHD paradigm is fairly consistent in pointing to the social difficulties that many kids labeled ADD/ADHD have with peers, teachers, and parents (Barkley, 1990). To help with these problems, experts in the field have created social skills programs designed to help these kids learn the art of making friends, how to recognize social cues, and how to deal with anger in relationships (Guevremont, 1990; Kolko, Loar, & Sturnick, 1990).

These programs are among the strongest and most helpful components of the ADD/ADHD paradigm. Yet, because they emerge out of a *deficit paradigm*, they tend to neglect the broader context within which to view the social behavior of many kids labeled ADD/ADHD, including the following:

- Not all kids labeled ADD/ADHD have social problems; some, in fact, are leaders, popular with friends, or naturally gregarious.
- Some kids who show social difficulties in school may demonstrate social skills in nonschool contexts: in community theater, volunteer roles, or even in nonsocially sanctioned activities such as gangs.
- Even among many kids who show clear social adjustment problems both inside and outside of school, their difficulties may stem more from their strong personalities, intense individualism, or the possession of a passionate nature, than from specific social deficiencies related to ADD/ADHD.

As noted in the "Positive Role Models" section, many highly creative and eminent people in history were not easy to get along with because they marched to the beat of a different drummer and existed outside of the social norm. In a similar way, many kids labeled ADD/ADHD who experience social problems may have interpersonal difficulties because they simply don't fit into the normal social conventions of what is considered acceptable behavior within particular social contexts (e.g., specific peer groups, school culture).

This does not excuse their need to fit in (especially because most children *would like* to fit in). These observations, however, suggest that we view the interpersonal situation somewhat differently from how ADD/ADHD experts would suggest: for example, not as deficits in social behavior, but rather as a "poor fit" or mismatch between the person and one or more specific social contexts.

Strategies like peer tutoring, class meetings, and engineering positive social occasions can help many students labeled ADD/ADHD learn new social skills and, at the same time, discover new social contexts within which they can function positively as the unique human beings they are.

Peer and Cross-Age Tutoring

One way of creating a new and more positive social context is through peer or cross-age tutoring. By pairing up a student labeled ADD/ADHD with a younger child (cross-age tutoring) to help with a specific activity (e.g., a reading or math skill), the student with attention or behavioral difficulties has to function as the responsible member of the relationship.

Through peer tutoring, an ADD/ADHD-labeled child can share a skill she knows how to do with a student of the same age who lacks that skill. In one program, a group of kids identified as having behavior problems successfully taught a group of kids labeled "gifted" how to use certain symbols in sign language (Osguthorpe, 1985). Programs like this turn labels on their head and redefine social contexts so that students can learn to see each other in new ways.

Finally, buddy programs, where an older student (with or without the ADD/ADHD label) takes a child labeled ADD/ADHD under his wing, can provide that child with a positive role model to learn acceptable forms of behavior (DuPaul & Henningson, 1993; Fiore & Becker, 1994).

Class Meetings

Consider setting aside regular class time to hold meetings based on William Glasser's educational ideas (Glasser, 1975; Glasser & Dotson, 1998). These meetings provide more opportunities to create special social settings within which students labeled ADD/ADHD can learn new kinds of social behavior and experience themselves as positive social beings.

Certainly, class meetings and other cooperative groups could be used simply as an opportunity for other students to complain about the behavior of these kids, only aggravating already problematic relationships. Run properly, however, a class meeting can provide opportunities for students labeled ADD/ADHD to get supportive feedback on how they are coming across to others, to receive social recognition for positive things they've done in class, to share their own constructive feelings and ideas about class issues, and to feel like an equal member of a total social unit.

Positive Social Moments

In addition to having regular class meetings, consider other ways in which you can create conditions within which positive social interactions can take place in school. Here are some examples:

- Let students labeled ADD/ADHD share a special interest with a class or teach the class something they know how to do well.
- Find other students you feel that this child would be compatible with, and group them together for certain class activities.
- Think about other social settings that you feel the student might experience some success in: class parties, after-school clubs or sports in the student's areas of interest or expertise, class sing-a-longs, or nature walks, for example.
- Be sure to establish positive rapport with the child yourself. Take a little time at the beginning of the day to talk personally to the student about his life, concerns, needs, and hopes for the day. At the end of the day, touch base with him again to review the day's events. Knowing that he has one reliable positive social relationship in school to serve as a kind of a touchstone may make it easier for him to venture forth into the often choppy social seas of school culture.

Ecological Strategies

The holistic approach taken in this book might well be regarded itself as ecological in nature (because it seeks to comprehend the broad terrain, so to speak, of a child's life, rather than simply the "potholes" or deficits). But the strategies listed here as "ecological" relate directly to specific aspects of the child's immediate environment: *space*, *time*, *food*, *sound*, and *color*.

By understanding the positive and negative effects that these environmental factors can have on the attention spans and behaviors of students labeled ADD/ADHD, educators can begin to modify the environment to reflect an optimum level of support for each student's unique ecological sensitivities.

Space

Most educators are familiar with studies where rats were placed in overcrowded conditions and responded by displaying greater evidence of aggressiveness (Weinstein, 1979). Other studies have attempted to link overcrowded housing to hyperactive behavior in some kids (Thomas, Chess, Sillen, & Menzez, 1974). Such findings certainly shouldn't be ignored when it comes to the classroom, especially in situations where students labeled ADD/ADHD may be required to learn in overcrowded classrooms. What Weinstein noted in 1979 still applies: "Nowhere else [but in schools] are large groups of individuals packed so closely together for so many hours, yet expected to perform at peak efficiency on difficult learning tasks and to interact harmoniously" (p. 585).

Even in classrooms that aren't overcrowded, teachers would do well to consider the importance of space as an ecological variable and help modify the classroom space to work in favor of kids who are labeled ADD/ADHD. Classroom design expert Anita Olds (1979) notes some of the problems in traditional classroom spaces:

> The barrenness and homogeneity of the physical parameters of classrooms can deaden arousal and interfere with children's capacities to stay alert and attentive. Cold, shiny tile floors, multiple chairs and tables of identical design and hard finish, dull-colored walls lacking recesses or changes in texture, ceilings of uniform height, which dwarf the size of the room's occupants, and fluorescent lights, which spread a constant high-powered glare over all activities indiscriminately, all contribute to feelings of boredom, listlessness, and dislike for the settings in which learning takes place (p. 95).

Forty years ago, educators put children identified as "hyperactive" into bare rooms in the belief that any extra stimulation would set them off (Cruickshank, 1975). As we've seen earlier in this book, however, research now suggests that many kids labeled ADD/ADHD may be *under*aroused and need a *high-stimulation* environment to calm them down (Zentall, 1993a and b; Zentall & Zentall, 1976). Bland classroom spaces, such as those described by Olds, may lead these students to seek stimulation through fidgeting, daydreaming, socializing, or wandering around to reach their optimal level of arousal.

Though I found no overall recommendation for structuring classroom space with children identified as ADD/ADHD, here are some suggestions that may be helpful for individual students:

• Allow students to configure their workspace in a way that permits them to express their individuality (e.g., through art designs and displays). Each student should feel that she has a space where she feels a sense of *ownership and belonging*.

• Provide different types of spaces in the classroom that are appropriate to different energy states (e.g., a private nook for quiet reflection, a social area for interpersonal interaction, a hands-on area for building things or creating projects) and use them to match a student's energy level to a specific space.

• Creating a variety of ways in which students can complete work (e.g., sitting, standing, lying down, working alone, working in pairs, working in groups), and provide the appropriate spaces for these types of configurations to work effectively.

• Enliven the classroom with plants and animals (e.g., potted plants, a gerbil cage, a terrarium).

• Where possible, substitute natural light and incandescent light for fluorescent lighting.

• Consider some of the following additions to help personalize classroom space: pillows, soft furniture, kid-sized furniture, mobiles, murals, carpets, canopies, and wall dividers.

In a classroom space that is inviting, stimulating, diverse, and personalized, students labeled ADD/ADHD may be less likely to feel that they need to create a space for themselves through hyperactive, impulsive, or distractible behaviors.

Time

An important new field of study called *chronopsychology* has raised awareness about how the ecological variable of time can affect learning and behavior. The most important temporal rhythms experienced by human beings are the *circadian rhythms* that occur in 24-hour solar and 25-hour lunar cycles. According to some authorities, overall alertness tends to rise through the morning in most people to a noonday high, and then declines steadily throughout the afternoon (Dolnick, 1992; Zagar & Bowers, 1983). Short-term memory appears to peak around nine in the morning for most people, while long-term memory seems to function best at around three in the afternoon. In studies with kids identified as ADD/ADHD or hyperactive, performances on a range of problem-solving tasks were better in the morning than in the afternoon, and restlessness appeared to reach its peak in the afternoon (Porrino et al., 1983). Some implications of these findings are as follows:

• Schedule activities requiring short-term memory (e.g., pop quizzes, drill, lecture, fact-based responses) and problem-solving (e.g., math tests, science experiments) in the morning hours.

• Plan open-ended experiences (e.g., reading for pleasure, art, music) and activities involving motor activity (e.g., hands-on projects, physical education, games) in the afternoon.

As Sylwester and Cho (1992/1993) write:

It makes sense to schedule curricular priorities that require rapt attention and precise response during the morning, when it's easier to maintain attention. It is also logical to schedule interesting activities that demand less precision and sustained attention in the afternoon, when students' inherent interest in the activity will elevate their attention level (p. 74).

Individual students, however, may not necessarily follow these broad patterns (Callan, 1997/1998). For some kids, it may be necessarily to keep a daily log on their behavior to determine which time of day tends to reflect their peak time of focused attention. Once this time of day has been identified, then material requiring sustained attention can be presented to these particular students during their best time of alertness.

Sound

Background noises in the classroom can serve to either enhance or disrupt the attention and behavior of students. In one study, S. Cohen, Evans, Krantz, Stokols, and Kelley (1981) looked at the performance of students at a school near Los Angeles International Airport—with the constant sound of planes flying overhead—and concluded that they were more likely to give up in frustration on academic tasks than a group of controls in schools not situated near airports.

Teachers should be aware of how other noises, such as the buzzing from fluorescent lights, the hum of school furnaces, and the noises from nearby factories or outside traffic, might serve as distractions for students labeled ADD/ADHD.

On the other hand, some sounds—especially music—may prove to enhance the learning environment for kids with attention and behavior difficulties. In some studies, rock music has been observed to calm down groups of students identified as hyperactive or ADD/ADHD (Cripe, 1986; Scott, 1969). In such cases, the background recordings appear to serve almost as a kind of "musical Ritalin," providing the extra stimulation required by some kids who have been labeled ADD/ADHD.

Of course, not all students diagnosed as ADD/ADHD will bene-fit—some may be highly distracted by music, or certain types of music or sounds. Several resources, however, point to the important effects of music on mood, behavior, and learning and provide musical selec-tions designed to evoke certain moods (Bonny & Savary, 1990; Lingerman, 1995). Consider exploring the potential of music to help focus attention and soothe distractible behavior. Here are some ideas for getting started:

• Experiment with different kinds of background music in the classroom, and notice which pieces seem to have the best effect on behavior and attention

• Start the day (or class) with music. This might simply be a musical piece to help center and calm, or a song that students sing together, or a live musical performance by students, parent volunteers, or others in the community.

• Provide a musical listening center in the classroom where stu-dents can listen to different types of music through earphones while studying without disturbing others.

• Consider using background music or a "white sound" machine to mask the sounds of chronic distractions (e.g., traffic, machinery) in the immediate environment.

By choosing the right sounds for the classroom, you can help "soothe the hyperactive breast" and create a harmonious learning environ-ment for all students.

Food

For at least some students identified as ADD/ADHD, it may be true to suggest that "what's eating Johnny is what Johnny's eating!" Like medications, food represents an aspect of children's environment that very literally becomes a part of their biological apparatus. As such, we need to consider its effect on attention and behavior, in any holistic approach to the ADD/ADHD question. For example, research has suggested that a balanced breakfast—that includes both protein and carbohydrates—helps students focus attention and limit restlessness (Conners, 1989).

Some research also supports the use of special diets with a small group of students within the total group identified as ADD/ADHD. For some students, the removal of foods that contain special chemical additives (including artificial flavorings, synthetic dyes, and certain preservatives such as BHA and BHT) and those foods that have naturally occurring salicylates (e.g., apricots, cherries, plums) may help lessen hyperactivity (Feingold, 1974; Hersey, 1996). Although such diets have come under fire from food industry groups, several well-designed studies indicate that certain kids show a dramatic behavioral improvement after the removal of these foods (Egger, Stolla, & McEwen, 1992; Kaplan, McNicol, Conte, & Moghadam, 1989).

Similarly, diets that seek to identify and remove allergenic foods from the diet—including such foods as chocolate, milk, wheat, or corn—have been shown to ameliorate the behavior problems of certain kids (Egger, Carter, Graham, Gumley, & Soothill, 1985).

One of the difficulties with special diets is that it is difficult to determine in advance who will benefit. These diets can also be hard to implement inasmuch as they require controlling all the food that goes into a child's mouth every day. With the approval and willingness of a child to undertake it, however, a special diet may be worth pursuing in individual cases.

Behavioral Strategies

The ADD/ADHD field has provided a wide range of techniques, methods, systems, programs, resources, and equipment based on Skinnerian principles of behavior modification (A.D.D. Warehouse,

1998). Although many of these programs and strategies are effective in changing behavior, most of them are used in an externally controlling way. Adults tell children what the rules are, and then reward the children with points, praise, or privileges, or "punish" them with "response costs" (e.g., removal of points, refusal of privileges). In such situations, students have little input into the whole process of behavior change.

Research suggests, however, that students labeled ADD/ADHD may become frustrated with the removal of points or privileges and have a harder time behaving (Douglas & Parry, 1994). Other research indicates that these kids may function more effectively when they have some control over their fate (Adelman, MacDonald, Nelson, Smith, & Taylor, 1990; Powell & Nelson, 1997). As a result, it may be far better to use behavioral strategies that *internally empower* students than those that externally control them.

The behavioral strategies listed here—collaborative discipline, student-chosen time out, and feedback—are intended to give students identified as ADHD a greater sense of ownership over their lives in helping to change attention and behavior. As such, they reach back to the original meaning of the word *discipline*, which is related to the Latin word *discipulus*, meaning "a learner." We essentially want our students not to change their behavior like robots, but to do so with understanding, reflection, and learning, so that they can begin to regulate their own lives.

Collaborative Discipline

Using a collaborative form of discipline, students have *input* into the rules of the classroom and into designing the rewards and "response costs" that will ensue if they do not follow the rules. In my own classroom for kids identified as having behavior problems, I switched over from an externally controlling reward system to this more collaborative approach over a period of several months. Before the new system was put into place, we spent hours discussing the rules and consequences for behavior. This process helped empower the kids immediately by providing them with opportunities to reflect on their behavior and its consequences in creating or inhibiting classroom harmony.

Teachers who fear giving up control to students in such a situation needn't fear, because the teacher does have final veto power over the resulting system (often my students would suggest very harsh punishments for rule-breakers, in some cases reflecting their own abusive home backgrounds). In my classroom, however, the students felt honored at having their own voices listened to and their input considered and used in the final outcome. When the collaborative system was in place, students immediately started breaking the rules, but they were *their* rules. Moreover, they had to face consequences that *they themselves* had helped to fashion. Consequently, the kind of friction or power struggle that can emerge between student and teacher from an externally controlling system, simply no longer existed. Students had to learn to live within a system that they themselves had created.

For information on creating discipline systems that empower rather than control, see Curwin and Mendler (1989), Kohn (1996), and Nelsen (1996).

Time Out

An excellent example of a behavior approach that can be used either as an externally controlling or internally empowering strategy is time out, where (in the externally controlling version) "noncompliant" children are told to go to a special area of the home or classroom for a designated number of minutes. This is the "dunce cap" area, or the rocking chair corner frequented by Dennis the Menace in the Sunday comics.

In one of the most popular behavior-modification programs used by ADD/ADHD educators and parents—"1–2–3–Magic!"—time out represents the key component (Phelan, 1996). When a child misbehaves or is "noncompliant," the teacher or parent is instructed to say "that's 1." If the student continues to misbehave or be noncompliant, the educator is told to say "that's 2." Finally, if the student doesn't obey, the parent or teacher says, "that's 3, take 5." And the student must spend five minutes in a time-out area.

The problem with this approach, or other time-out systems like it, is that students must go to an area with very little stimulation (usually a chair in an empty corner of the room) and simply wait there with nothing to do. Some teachers tell students to go to the time out area and "Think!" These generalized instructions, however, are rarely effective in providing a stimulus to help students right the wrongs they have committed. Instead of "thinking," more often students will be daydreaming, fuming about the injustices that have been served upon them, planning strategies of revenge, fidgeting, throwing spitballs across the room at classmates, and engaging in other forms of disruptive behavior (which may earn them more time in the corner).

Zentall and Zentall (1983) suggest that traditional time-out areas may not best serve the needs of students labeled ADD/ADHD inasmuch as these areas are stimulus-poor and thus do not provide the extra stimulation that many kids labeled ADD/ADHD require to reach their optimal level of arousal. As a result, these kids provide their own stimulation in the time-out center, in a way that is often disruptive to the classroom.

Nelsen and Glenn (1991) have proposed an internally empowering way of using time out as a behavioral strategy. They recommend letting the child decide when it's time to go to the time-out area. They suggest giving the child a timer so that he can set and monitor the amount of time he needs to get himself together, and even letting the student select the location of the time-out area, giving it a special name that doesn't have punitive connotations (e.g., the "quiet space," "home base," "centering spot").

To provide stimulation in such a center, consider some of the following resources:

• Books and recordings on discipline issues for children.

• Writing and drawing materials so that they can creatively express their own feelings about what happened.

• Games designed to help students learn effective coping strategies.

One teacher called her area "the office" and let kids use it in other ways besides "time out" so that it was associated with positive learning experiences. Used in this internally empowering way, time out can serve as an important vehicle—not for punishing noncompliance— but for teaching new and more constructive patterns of behavior.

Behavioral Feedback

Many students who misbehave in school have little awareness of their actions or how those actions affect those around them. In such cases, providing immediate behavioral feedback can be a highly effective approach to help reflect a student's behavior back to them in a way they can directly experience. Here are a few ways to structure behavioral feedback in the classroom:

• Select a specific behavior (e.g., "falling" out of the desk) and count the number of times a student does this during the day. At the end of the day, give the student a slip of paper with this information (e.g., "Today, you fell out of your desk 5 times."). Make sure to do this without comment. Do this for a number of days. Once the student is accustomed to this approach, have him keep track of his own behavior.

- Take a photo, or make a videotape or audiotape, that catches the disturbing behavior in progress. Then, show this to the student in a nonjudgmental way (apart from the other students). Or make a video of the child, cutting out the undesirable behaviors and showing only the kinds of behavior you wish to see. Then show this to the student (Walther & Beare, 1991; Woltersdorf, 1992).

- Trade places with the student, so that the student is seated in the teacher's chair, and you are in the child's seat. Then, imitate some of the student's problematic types of behavior (again, it's best to do this apart from the other students). Discuss with the student what it is like to see his own behavior from the teacher's vantage point.

It's important to do these feedback techniques in a nonmocking, nonjudgmental way. Avoid following up the feedback with long sermons on proper behavior, or admonitions about how to properly behave. By simply providing students with this direct information, you're essentially asking them, "Is this how you want to come across to the world?"

Biological Strategies

Teachers might wonder what sorts of biological strategies they could possibly use in the classroom. Certainly the first interventions that come to mind in this category are psychoactive medications, such as Ritalin; and these are properly outside the province of the educator, and within the purview of the prescribing physician. I want to mention them here, however, because they do represent another set of tools that can be used to help children in situations like the following:

• Children whose problems are particularly biological in nature (e.g., where there has been specific brain damage due to illness or accident).

• Children in acute behavioral crisis, where chronic unremitting symptoms require immediate interventions (McGuinness, 1985, p. 229; Turecki, 1989, p. 231).

• Children for whom nonmedical interventions have been tried and failed to be effective (American Academy of Pediatrics, 1987).

At the same time, I'd like to suggest that there are other biological interventions teachers can use in the schools (or suggest to parents). These interventions are not drug related, yet do have a positive biological impact. The most prominent set of such strategies involves the use of food (discussed on pp. 95–96). Seen in the proper context, food actually represents a wide range of "drugs" that we safely ingest every day. Understanding how different foods affect the brain can give us a better understanding of how we can help improve a child's behavioral chemistry.

It is possible to view most of the other interventions in this book as having a potentially positive effect on a student's psychobiological integrity. With accumulating evidence from brain science regarding the effect of the environment on the growing brain (e.g., Diamond & Hopson, 1998), it's becoming more clear that everything a teacher uses in the classroom—whether it be computers, music, hands-on instruction, cooperative learning, visual thinking, role play, or any of the other ideas suggested in this book and elsewhere—has its own effect on a child's brain, creating new neuronal connections and enriching the child's neurochemistry in other ways, as well (e.g., Jensen, 1998; Sylwester, 1995).

EPILOGUE

We come now to the end of this book; and as we do, I think it would be helpful to make some general comments. First, it appears that despite the many inconsistencies and anomalies that I've suggested in this book, the ADD/ADHD paradigm shows no immediate signs of shifting into the more broadly based paradigm that I've envisioned in the course of these pages. In fact, quite the reverse appears to be true. ADD/ADHD seems to be growing as an explanatory vehicle for children's difficulties, just as our entire culture is becoming more insistent on reducing virtually every aspect of human life to genetics and the movement of chemicals and electrical impulses in the brain.

As I pointed out at the end of Chapter 3, the brain is certainly important to everything we do, and we do carry it around with us wherever we go! However, to see it as the fixed point around which everything revolves (the neurological equivalent of a medieval "earth-centered" or Ptolemaic paradigm) is, in my view, limited. What I am perhaps arguing for in this book is a sort of Copernican shift in our attitude toward children who have trouble attending and behaving. I'm arguing that we see the biological, not as the center of the universe, but rather as one of several "planets" orbiting around a solar body, who in my metaphor here is represented by the whole child, the "radiant child," humanity's most important natural energy source!

It's interesting to note that in some of the perspectives that I did not include in this book, the child labeled hyperactive or ADD is positively viewed as an intense soul or spirit attempting to express itself in the woefully limited structure of a human body or a stifling social system (see Hartmann, 1997; Hillman, 1997; Inayat Khan, 1960;

Steiner, 1974). I'd like to leave you with the thought that these children whom we've labeled ADD or ADHD do, in fact, represent an important energy source that may at present be a light under a bushel, or a laser beam wreaking havoc, or an experiment in nuclear fusion gone awry, but that properly understood, nourished, and channeled, can truly light our world!

REFERENCES

Abikoff, H. (1985). Efficacy of cognitive training interventions in hyperactive children: A critical review. *Clinical Psychology Review, 5*(5), 479–512.

Abikoff, H., & Gittelman, R. (1985). The normalizing effects of methylphenidate on the classroom behavior of ADD-H children. *Journal of Abnormal Child Psychology, 13*(1), 33–44.

A.D.D. Warehouse. (1998). *Catalog.* Plantation, FL: Author.

Adelman, H. S., MacDonald, V. M., Nelson, P., Smith, D. C., & Taylor, L. (1990). Motivational readiness and the participation of children with learning and behavior problems in psychoeducational decision making. *Journal of Learning Disabilities, 23*(3), 171–176.

Alexander, J. (1990, April). Hyperactive children: Which sports have the right stuff? *The Physician and Sportsmedicine, 18,* 106.

Allender, J. S. (1991). *Imagery in teaching and learning.* New York: Praeger.

American Academy of Pediatrics. (1987, November). Medication for children with an attention deficit disorder. *Pediatrics, 80,* 758.

American Psychiatric Association. (1994). *Diagnostic and statistical manual of mental disorders (DSM-IV).* Washington, DC: American Psychiatric Press.

Ames, L. B. (1985). Learning disability—very big around here. *Research Communications on Psychology, Psychiatry, and Behavior, 10*(142), 17–34.

Armstrong, T. (1987a). Describing strengths in children identified as "learning disabled" using Howard Gardner's theory of multiple intelligences as an organizing framework. *Dissertation Abstracts International, 48,* 08A (University Microfilms No. 87-25, 844).

Armstrong, T. (1987b). *In their own way: Discovering and encouraging your child's personal learning style.* New York: Tarcher/Putnam.

Armstrong, T. (1988). Learning differences—not disabilities. *Principal, 68*(1), 34–36.

Armstrong, T. (1994). *Multiple intelligences in the classroom.* Alexandria, VA: Association for Supervision and Curriculum Development.

Armstrong, T. (1997). *The myth of the A.D.D. child: 50 ways to improve your child's behavior and attention span without drugs, labels, or coercion.* New York: Plume.

Arnsten, A. F. T. (1999). Development of the cerebral cortex: XIV. Stress impairs prefrontal cortical function. *Journal of the American Academy of Child and Adolescent Psychiatry, 38*(2), 220–222.

Barker, J. A. (1993). *Paradigms: The business of discovering the future.* New York: Harperbusiness.

Barkley, R. (1990). *Attention deficit hyperactivity disorder: A handbook for diagnosis and treatment.* New York: Guilford Press.

Barkley, R. (1995). *Taking charge of ADHD: The complete, authoritative guide for parents.* New York: Guilford Press.

Begley, S. (1996, January 15). Holes in those genes. *Newsweek,* 57.

Bender, R. L., & Bender, W. N. (1996). *Computer-assisted instruction for students at risk for ADHD, mild disabilities, or academic problems.* Needham Heights, MA: Allyn & Bacon.

Benson, H., & Klipper, M. Z. (1990). *The relaxation response*. New York: Avon.

Berk, L. E., & Landau, S. (1993). Private speech of learning disabled and normally achieving children in classroom academic and laboratory contexts. *Child Development, 64*(2), 556–571.

Berk, L. E., & Potts, M. (1991). Development and functional significance of private speech among attention-deficit hyperactivity disordered and normal boys. *Journal of Abnormal Child Psychology, 19*(3), 357–377.

Berke, R. L. (1992, July 11). Sound bites grow at CBS, then vanish. *The New York Times*, p. L7.

Berlin, E. (1989, October). Michael's orchestra. *Ladies Home Journal*, p. 108.

Berthrong, J. H. (1994). *All under Heaven: Transforming paradigms in Confucian-Christian dialogue*. New York: SUNY Press.

Biederman, J., Newcorn, J., & Sprich, S. (1991). Comorbidity of attention deficit hyperactivity disorder with conduct, depressive, anxiety, and other disorders. *American Journal of Psychiatry, 148*(5), 564–577.

Biederman, J., Milberger, S., Faraone, S. V., Kiely, K., Guite, J., Mick, E., Ablon, S., Warburton, R., & Reed, E. (1995). Family-environment risk factors for attention-deficit hyperactivity disorder. *Archives of General Psychiatry, 52*, 464–469.

Blakeslee, S. (1997, September 2). Some biologists ask "Are genes everything?" *The New York Times*, pp. B1, B13.

Block, G. (1977). Hyperactivity: A cultural perspective. *Journal of Learning Disabilities, 10*(4), 48–52.

Bonny, H., & Savary, L. M. (1990). *Music and your mind*. Barrytown, NY: Station Hill Press.

Braswell, L., Bloomquist, M., & Pederson, S. (1991). *ADHD: A guide to understanding and helping children with attention deficit hyperactivity disorder in school settings*. Minneapolis: University of Minnesota.

Breggin, P. (1998). *Talking back to Ritalin: What doctors aren't telling you about stimulants for children*. Monroe, ME: Common Courage Press.

Brooks, R. B. (1992, Fall/Winter). Fostering self-esteem in children with ADD: The search for islands of competence. *CHADDER*, 12–15.

Brooks, R. B. (1994). Children at risk: Fostering resilience and hope. *American Journal of Orthopsychiatry, 64*(4), 545–553.

Budd, L. (1993). *Living with the active alert child: Groundbreaking strategies for parents*. Seattle, WA: Parenting Press.

Callan, R. J. (1997, December–1998, January). Giving students the (right) time of day. *Educational Leadership, 55*, 84–87.

Cameron, J. (1978). Parental treatment, children's temperament, and the risk of childhood behavioral problems. *American Journal of Orthopsychiatry, 48*(1), 140–141.

Campbell, L., Campbell, B., & Dickinson, D. (1996). *Teaching and learning through multiple intelligences*. Needham Heights, MA: Allyn & Bacon.

Carlson, E. A., Jacobvitz, D., & Sroufe, L. A. (1995). A developmental investigation of inattentiveness and hyperactivity. *Child Development, 66*(1), 37–54.

Cartwright, S. A. (1851, May). Report on the diseases and physical peculiarities of the Negro race. *The New-Orleans Medical and Surgical Journal, 7*, 691–716.

Castellanos, F. X., Lau, E., Tayebi, N., Lee, P., Long, R. E., Giedd, J. N., Sharp, W., Marsh, W. L., Walter, J. M., Hamburger, S. D., Ginns, E. I., Rapoport, J. L., & Sidranskyl, E. (1998). Lack of an association between a dopamine-4 receptor polymorphism and attention-deficit/hyperactivity disorder: Genetic and brain morphometric analyses. *Molecular Psychiatry, 3*(5), 431–434.

Ceci, S. J., & Tishman, J. (1984). Hyperactivity and incidental memory: Evidence for attention diffusion. *Child Development, 55*(6), 2192–2203.

CH.A.D.D. (1994). Attention deficit disorders: An educator's guide. *CH.A.D.D. Facts 5*. Plantation, FL: Author.

Chess, S., & Thomas, A. (1996). *Temperament: Theory and practice.* New York: Brunner/Mazel.

Christensen, A., Phillips, S., Glasgow, R. E., & Johnson, S. M. (1983). Parental characteristics and interactional dysfunction in families with child behavior problems: A preliminary investigation. *Journal of Abnormal Child Psychology, 11*(1), 153–166.

Coat, T. (1982, January 13). Can running help troubled kids? *The San Diego Tribune,* p. A1.

Cohen, M. W. (1997). *The attention zone: A parent's guide to attention deficit/hyperactivity disorder.* New York: Brunner-Mazel.

Cohen, S., Evans, G. W., Krantz, D. S., Stokols, D., & Kelly, S. (1981). Aircraft noise and children: Longitudinal and cross-sectional evidence on adaptation to noise and the effectiveness of noise abatement. *Journal of Personality and Social Psychology, 40,* 331–345.

Conners, C. K. (1989). *Feeding the brain: How foods affect children.* New York: Plenum.

Corrigall, R., & Ford, T. (1996). Methylphenidate euphoria. *Journal of the American Academy of Child and Adolescent Psychiatry, 35*(1), 1421.

Conrad, P. (1975). The discover of hyperkinesis: Notes on the medicalization of deviant behavior. *Social Problems, 23*(1), 12–21.

Cowart, V. S. (1988). The Ritalin controversy: What's made this drug's opponents hyperactive? *Journal of the American Medical Association, 259*(17), 2521–2523.

Cramond, B. (1994). Attention-deficit hyperactivity disorder and creativity: What is the connection? *Journal of Creative Behavior, 28*(2), 193–210.

Cripe, F. F. (1986). Rock music as therapy for children with attention deficit disorder: An exploratory study. *Journal of Music Therapy, 23*(1), 30–37.

Cruickshank, W. M. (1975). The learning environment. In W. M. Cruickshank & D. P. Hallahan (Eds.), *Perceptual and learning disabilities in children: Vol. 1. Psychoeducational practices.* Syracuse, NY: Syracuse University Press.

Curwin, R. L., & Mendler, A. N. (1989). *Discipline with dignity.* Alexandria, VA: Association for Supervision and Curriculum Development.

Dang, T. T. (1994). *Beginning t'ai chi.* New York: Charles Tuttle.

Davidson, P. (1996). *Super source for Cuisenaire Rods.* White Plains, NY: Cuisenaire Company of America.

Diamond, M., & Hopson, J. (1998). *Magic trees of the mind.* New York: Dutton.

Diller, L. H. (1998). *Running on Ritalin: A physician reflects on children, society, and performance in a pill.* New York: Bantam/Doubleday/Dell.

Diller, L. H., & Tanner, J. (1996). Etiology of ADHD: Nature or nurture? *American Journal of Psychiatry, 153*(3), 451–452.

Divoky, D. (1989). Ritalin: Education's fix-it drug? *Phi Delta Kappan, 70*(8), 599–605 .

Dolnick, E. (1992, April 19). Snap out of it! *San Francisco Chronicle*, p. 9.

Douglas, V. I., & Parry, P. A. (1994). Effects of reward and nonreward on frustration and attention in attention deficit disorder. *Journal of Abnormal Child Psychology, 22*(3), 281–301.

Dreikurs, R., & Soltz, V. (1964). *Children the challenge*. New York: Hawthorne.

Druckman, D., & Swets, J. A. (Eds.). (1988). *Enhancing human performance: Issues, theories, and techniques*. Washington, DC: National Academy Press.

Drug Enforcement Administration. (1995, October). *Methylphenidate: A background paper*. Washington, DC: U.S. Department of Justice.

Duckworth, E. (1979). Either we're too early and they can't learn it or we're too late and they know it already: The dilemma of applying Piaget. *Harvard Educational Review, 49*(3), 297–312.

Dunn, F. M., & Howell, R. J. (1986). Relaxation training and its relationship to hyperactivity in boys. *Journal of Clinical Psychology, 38*(1), 92–100.

DuPaul, G. J., & Henningson, P. N. (1993). Peer tutoring effects on the classroom performance of children with attention deficit hyperactivity disorder. *School Psychology Review, 22*(1), 134–143.

Dyment, P. G. (1990). Hyperactivity, stimulants, and sports. *The Physician and Sportsmedicine, 18*(4), 22.

Dyson, A. H. (1987). The value of "Time off task": Young children's spontaneous talk and deliberate text. *Harvard Educational Review, 57*(4), 396–420.

Eddowes, E. A., Aldridge, J., & Culpepper, S. (1994). Primary teachers' classroom practices and their perceptions of children's attention problems. *Perceptual and Motor Skills, 79*(2), 787–790.

Egger, J., Carter, C. M., Graham, P. J., Gumley, D., & Soothill, J. M. (1985, March 9). Controlled trial of oligoantigenic treatment in the hyperkinetic syndrome. *The Lancet, 1*(8428), 540–545.

Egger, J., Stolla, A., & McEwen, L. M. (1992, May 9). Controlled trial of hyposensitisation in children with food-induced hyperkinetic syndrome. *The Lancet, 339*(8802), 1150–1153.

Elkind, D. (1981). *The hurried child: Growing up too fast too soon*. Reading, MA: Addison-Wesley.

Elkind, D. (1984). *All grown up and no place to go: Teenagers in crisis*. Reading, MA: Addison-Wesley.

Elkind, D. (1988). *Miseducation: Preschoolers at risk*. New York: Alfred A. Knopf.

Elmer-DeWitt, P. (1990, November 26). Why junior won't sit still. *Time*, 59.

Erikson, E. (1977). *Toys and reasons*. New York: W. W. Norton.

Ernst, M., Liebenauer, L. L., King, A. C., Fitzgerald, G. A., Cohen, R. M., & Zametkin, A. J. (1994). Reduced brain metabolism in hyperactive girls. *Journal of the American Academy of Child and Adolescent Psychiatry, 33*(6), 858–868.

Fehlings, D. L., Roberts, W., Humphries, T., & Dawes, G. (1991). Attention deficit hyperactivity disorder: Does cognitive behavioral therapy improve home behavior? *Journal of Developmental and Behavioral Pediatrics, 12*(4), 223–228.

Feingold, B. (1974). *Why your child is hyperactive*. New York: Random House.

Fiore, T. A., & Becker, E. A. (1994). *Promising classroom interventions for students with attention deficit disorder.* Research Triangle Park, NC: Center for Research in Education.

Fleisher, L. S., Soodak, L. C., & Jelin, J. A. (1984). Selective attention deficits in learning disabled children: Analysis of the data base. *Exceptional Children, 51*(2) 136–141.

Ford, M. J., Poe, V., & Cox, J. (1993). Attending behaviors of ADHD children in math and reading using various types of software. *Journal of Computing in Childhood Education, 4*(2), 183–196.

Foster, W. (1986). *Paradigms and promises: New approaches to educational administration.* New York: Prometheus.

Freed, J., & Parsons, L. (1998). *Right-brained children in a left-brained world: Unlocking the potential of your ADD child.* New York: Fireside.

Fuller, R., Walsh, P. N., & McGinley, P. (Eds.). (1997). *A century of psychology: Progress, paradigms and prospects for the new millennium.* New York: Routledge.

Furman, R. (1996). Correspondence. *Journal of Child Psychotherapy, 22*(1), 157–160.

Gallas, K. (1994). *The languages of learning: How children talk, write, dance, draw, and sing their understanding of the world.* New York: Teachers College Press.

Galvin, M. (1988). *Otto learns about his medicine.* New York: Brunner/Mazel.

Garber, S. W., Garber, M. D., & Spizman, R. F. (1997). *Beyond Ritalin: Facts about medication and other strategies for helping children, adolescents, and adults with attention deficit disorders.* New York: HarperCollins.

Gardner, H. (1983). *Frames of mind: The theory of multiple intelligences.* New York: Basic Books.

Gardner, H. (1993). *Multiple intelligences: The theory in practice.* New York: Basic Books.

Gehret, J. (1991). *Eagle eye: A child's guide to paying attention.* Fairport, NY: Verbal Images Press.

Gibbs, N. (1998, November 28). The age of Ritalin. *Time, 152,* 86–96.

Giedd, J. N., Castellanos, F. X., Casey, B. J., Kozuch, P., King, A. C., Hamburger, S. D., & Rapoport, J. L. (1994, May). Quantitative morphology of the corpus callosum in attention deficit hyperactivity disorder. *American Journal of Psychiatry, 151*(5), 665–669.

Glasser, W. (1975). *Schools without failure.* New York: HarperCollins.

Glasser, W., & Dotson, K. L. (1998). *Choice theory in the classroom.* New York: HarperPerennial.

Glusker, A. (1997, March 30). Deficit selling. *The Washington Post Magazine,* 13–16, 25–27.

Goertzel, V., & Goertzel, M. G. (1962). *Cradles of eminence.* Boston: Little, Brown & Co.

Goldenberg, I., & Goldenberg, H. (1980). *Family therapy: An overview* (3rd ed.). Monterey, CA: Brooks-Cole.

Goldman, L. S., Genel, M., Bezman, R. J., & Slanetz, P. J. (1998, April 8). Diagnosis and treatment of attention-deficit/hyperactivity disorder in children and adolescents. *Journal of the American Medical Association, 279*(14), 1100–1107.

Goleman, D. (1996). *The meditative mind: Varieties of meditative experience.* New York: Tarcher/Putnam.

Goodman, G., & Poillion, M. J. (1992). ADD: Acronym for any dysfunction or difficulty. *The Journal of Special Education, 26*(1), 37–56.

Gordon, M. (1995, Fall). Certainly not a fad, but it can be over-diagnosed. *Attention!* 20–22.

Gould, S. J. (1975). The child as man's real father. *Natural History, 84*(5), 18–22.

Gould, S. J. (1981). *The mismeasure of man.* New York: Norton.

Green, C., & Chee, K. (1998). *Understanding ADHD: Attention deficit hyperactivity disorder.* New York: Fawcett.

Greenspan, S. (1996). *The challenging child: Understanding, raising, and enjoying the five difficult types of children.* New York: Perseus Press.

Grinspoon, L., & Singer, S. B. (1973). Amphetamines in the treatment of hyperkinetic children. *Harvard Educational Review, 43*(4), 515–555.

Griss, S. (1998). *Minds in motion: A kinesthetic approach to teaching elementary curriculum.* Portsmouth, NH: Heinemann.

Guevremont, D. (1990). Social skills and peer relationship training. In R. Barkley (Ed.), *Attention deficit hyperactivity disorder: A handbook for diagnosis and treatment.* New York: Guilford Press.

Haggerty, B. (1995). *Nurturing intelligences: A guide to multiple intelligences theory and teaching.* Menlo Park, CA: Addison-Wesley.

Hales, D., & Hales, R. E. (1996, January 7). Finally, I know what's wrong. *Parade Magazine,* 10–11.

Hallowell, E. M., & Ratey, J. J. (1994a). *Driven to distraction.* New York: Pantheon.

Hallowell, E. M., & Ratey, J. J. (1994b). *Answers to distraction.* New York: Pantheon.

Hamlett, K. W., Pellegrini, D. S., & Conners, C. K. (1987). An investigation of executive processes in the problem-solving of attention deficit disorder-hyperactive children. *Journal of Pediatric Psychology, 12*(2), 227–240.

Hancock, L. (1996, March 18). Mother's little helper. *Newsweek, 127,* 50–59.

Hannaford, C. (1995). *Smart moves: Why learning is not all in your head.* Arlington, VA: Great Ocean.

Harris, M. J., Milich, R., Corbitt, E. M., Hoover, D. W., & Brady, M. (1992). Self-fulfilling effects of stigmatizing information on children's social interactions. *Journal of Personality and Social Psychology, 63*(1), 41–50.

Hartmann, T. (1997). *Attention deficit disorder: A different perception.* Grass Valley, CA: Underwood Books.

Hartocollis, A. (1998, November 21). Federal officials say study shows racial bias in special-education placement. *The New York Times,* p. A13.

Hauser, P., Zametkin, A. J., Martinez, P., Vitiello, B., Matochik, J. A., Mixson, A. J., & Weintraub, B. D. (1993). Attention deficit-hyperactivity disorder in people with generalized resistance to thyroid hormone. *New England Journal of Medicine, 328*(14), 997–1001.

Healy, J. (1991). *Endangered minds: Why our children don't think.* New York: Touchstone.

Healy, J. (1998). *Failure to connect: How computers affect our children's minds—for better and worse..* New York: Simon & Schuster.

Heilveil, I., & Clark, D. (1990, August). *Personality correlates of attention deficit hyperac-*

tivity disorder. Paper presented at the Annual Convention of the American Psychological Association, Boston, MA. (ERIC ED 331269)

Hersey, J. (1996). *Why can't my child behave?* Alexandria, VA: Pear Tree Press.

Heusmann, L. R., & Eron, L. D. (Eds.). (1986). *Television and the aggressive child: A cross-national comparison*. Hillsdale, NJ: Lawrence Erlbaum.

Hill, J. C., & Schoener, E. P. (1996). Age-dependent decline of attention deficit hyperactivity disorder. *American Journal of Psychiatry, 154*(9), 1323–1325.

Hillman, J. (1997). *The soul's code: In search of character and calling*. New York: Warner Books.

Hobbs, N. (1975). *The futures of children*. San Francisco: Jossey-Bass.

Houston, J. (1982). *The possible human*. New York: Tarcher/Putnam.

Hubbard, R., & Wald, E. (1993). *Exploding the gene myth*. Boston: Beacon Press.

Illich, I. (1976). *Medical nemesis*. New York: Bantam.

Inayat Khan. (1960). *The Sufi message of Hazrat Inayat Khan*. London: Barrie & Jenkins.

Ingersoll, B. D. (1988). *Your hyperactive child: A parent's guide to coping with attention deficit disorder*. New York: Doubleday.

Ingersoll, B. (1995, Fall). ADD: Not just another fad. *Attention!* 17–19.

Ingersoll, B. D., & Goldstein, S. (1993). *Attention deficit disorder and learning disabilities: Realities, myths, and controversial treatments*. New York: Doubleday.

Iyengar, B. K. S. (1995). *Light on yoga*. New York: Schocken Books.

Jacob, R. G., O'Leary, K. D., & Rosenblad, C. (1978). Formal and informal classroom settings: effects on hyperactivity. *Journal of Abnormal Child Psychology, 6*(1), 47–59.

Jensen, E. (1998). *Teaching with the brain in mind*. Alexandria, VA: Association for Supervision and Curriculum Development.

Johnson, T. M. (1997, July). Evaluating the hyperactive child in your office: Is it ADHD? *American Family Physician, 56*(1), 155–160.

Jung, C. G. (1981). *The development of personality*. Princeton, NJ: Princeton University Press.

Kaplan, B. J., McNicol, J., Conte, R. A., & Moghadam, H. K. (1989, January). Dietary replacement in preschool-aged hyperactive boys. *Pediatrics, 83*, 7–17.

Klein, R. G., & Mannuzza, S. (1991). Long-term outcome of hyperactive children: A review. *Journal of the American Academy of Child and Adolescent Psychiatry, 30*(3), 383–387.

Kohn, A. (1996). *Beyond discipline: From compliance to community*. Alexandria, VA: Association for Supervision and Curriculum Development.

Kolata, G. (1990, November 15). Hyperactivity is linked to brain abnormality. *The New York Times*, p. A1.

Kolko, D. J., Loar, L. L., & Sturnick, D. (1990). Inpatient social-cognitive skills training groups with conduct disordered and attention deficit disordered children. *Journal of Child Psychology & Psychiatry & Allied Disciplines, 31*(5), 737–748.

Kratter, J., & Hogan, J. D. (1982). *The use of meditation in the treatment of attention deficit disorder with hyperactivity*. (ERIC ED 232-787)

Krechevsky, M. (1991, February). Project spectrum: An innovative assessment alternative. *Educational Leadership, 48*, 43–49.

Kuhn, T. S. (1970). *The structure of scientific revolutions* (2nd ed.). Chicago: University of Chicago Press.

Kurcinka, M. (1992). *Raising your spirited child*. New York: HaperPerennial.

LaHoste, G. J., Swanson, J. M., Wigal, S. B., Glabe, C., Wigal, T., King, N., & Kennedy, J. L. (1996). Dopamine D4 receptor gene polymorphism is associated with attention deficit hyperactivity disorder. *Molecular Psychiatry, 1*, 121–124.

Landau, S., Lorch, E. P., & Milich, R. (1992). Visual attention to and comprehension of television in attention-deficit hyperactivity disordered and normal boys. *Child Development, 63*, 928–937.

Lazear, D. (1991). *Seven ways of knowing: Teaching for multiple intelligences*. Palatine, IL: Skylight.

Lazear, D. (1993). *Seven pathways of learning: Teaching students and parents about multiple intelligences*. Tucson, AZ: Zephyr Press.

Lazear, D. (1994). *Multiple intelligence approaches to assessment: Solving the assessment conundrum*. Tucson, AZ: Zephyr Press.

Lee, S. W. (1991). Biofeedback as a treatment for childhood hyperactivity: A critical review of the literature. *Psychological Reports, 68*(1), 163–192.

Levine, M. (1992). *All kinds of minds*. Cambridge, MA: Educators Publishing Services.

Lingerman, H. A. (1995). *The healing energies of music*. Wheaton, IL: Quest.

Linn, R. T., & Hodge, G. K. (1982). Locus of control in childhood hyperactivity. *Journal of Consulting and Clinical Psychology, 50*(4), 592–593.

Locher, P. J. (1995). Use of haptic training to modify impulse and attention control deficits of learning disabled children. *Journal of Learning Disabilities, 18*(2), 89–93.

Long, P., & Bowen, J. (1995, March). *Teaching students to take control of their learning*. Paper presented at the International Conference of the Learning Disabilities Association, Orlando, FL. (ERIC ED381989)

Lowenfeld, V. (1987). *Creative and mental growth* (8th ed.). New York: Macmillan.

Lozanov, G. (1978). *Suggestology and outlines of suggestopedy*. New York: Gordon & Breach.

Lubar, J., & Lubar, J. F. (1984). Electroencephalographic biofeedback of SMR and beta for treatment of attention deficit disorders in a clinical setting. *Biofeedback and Self Regulation, 9*(1), 1–23.

Lynn, R. (1979). *Learning disabilities: An overview of theories, approaches, and politics*. New York: The Free Press.

Machan, D. (1996, August 12). An agreeable affliction. *Forbes*, 148–151.

Malhatra, A. K., Virkkunen, M., Rooney, W., Eggert, M., Linnoila, M., & Goldman, D. (1996). The association between the dopamine D4 receptor (D4DR) 16 amino acid repeat polymorphism and novelty seeking. *Molecular Psychiatry, 1*(5), 388–391.

Mann, D. (1996). Serious play. *Teachers College Record, 97*(3), 116–169.

Mann, E. M., Ikeda, Y., Mueller, C. W., Takahashi, A., Tao, K. T., Humris, E., Li, B. L., & Chin, D. (1992). Cross-cultural differences in rating hyperactive-disruptive behaviors in children. *American Journal of Psychiatry, 149*(11), 1539–1542.

Manning, A. (1995, March 14). '90's teens find a new high by abusing Ritalin. *USA Today*, p. D1.

Mannuzza, S., Klein, R. G., Bessler, A., Malloy, P., & LaPadula, M. (1993). Adult out-come of hyperactive boys. *Archives of General Psychiatry, 50,* 565–576.

Margulies, N. (1991). *Mapping inner space: Learning and teaching mind mapping.* Tucson, AZ: Zephyr Press.

Markowitz, N. (1986, October). David was always on the move. *Learning, 15*(3), 53–54.

Maugh, T. H. (1996, May 1). Gene is a factor in hyperactivity, researchers say. *The Los Angeles Times,* Home Edition, Part A.

McBurnett, K., Lahey, B. B., & Pfiffner, L. J. (1993). Diagnosis of attention deficit disor-ders in DSM-IV: Scientific basics and implications for education. *Exceptional Children, 60*(2), 108–117.

McGee, R., & Share, D. L. (1988). Attention deficit disorder-hyperactivity and academ-ic failure: Which comes first and what should be treated? *Journal of the American Academy of Child and Adolescent Psychiatry, 27*(3), 318–325.

McGoldrick, M., & Gerson, R. (1986). *Genograms in family assessment.* New York: W. W. Norton.

McGuinness, D. (1985). *When children don't learn.* New York: BasicBooks.

McGuinness, D. (1989). Attention deficit disorder: The emperor's clothes, animal 'pharm' and other fiction. In S. Fisher & R. P. Greenberg (Eds.), *The limits of biolog-ical treatments for psychological distress* (pp. 151–183). Hillsdale, NJ: Lawrence Erlbaum.

Milich, R., & Okazaki, M. (1991). An examination of learned helplessness among atten-tion-deficit hyperactivity disordered boys. *Journal of Abnormal Child Psychology, 19*(5), 607–623.

Millman, P. G. (1984). The effects of computer-assisted instruction on attention deficits, achievement, and attitudes of learning-disabled children *Dissertation Abstracts International, 45,* 3114A.

Montagu, A. (1983). *Growing young.* New York: McGraw-Hill.

Moses, S. (1990a, February). Hypotheses on ADHD debated at conference. *APA Monitor,* 34.

Moses, S. (1990b, November). Unusual coalition nixes inclusion of A.D.D. in bill. *APA Monitor,* 37.

Moses, S. (1991, December). Letter on A.D.D. kids gets mixed reactions. *APA Monitor,* 36–37.

Moses-Zirkes, S. (1992, October). Path to kindergarten can be treacherous. *APA Monitor,* 52.

Moss, R. A. (1990). *Why Johnny can't concentrate: Coping with attention deficit problems.* New York: Bantam.

Mulligan, S. (1996). An analysis of score patterns of children with attention disorders on the sensory integration and praxis tests. *American Journal of Occupational Therapy, 50*(8), 647–654.

Murdock, M. (1989). *Spinning inward: Using guided imagery with children for learning cre-ativity, and relaxation.* Boston: Shambhala.

Napier, A. Y., & Whitaker, C. (1988). *The family crucible: The intense experience of family therapy.* New York: HarperPerennial.

Nathan, W. A. (1992). Integrated multimodal therapy of children with attention-deficit hyperactivity disorder. *Bulletin of the Menninger Clinic, 56*(3), 283–311.

Nelsen, J. (1996). *Positive discipline*. New York: Ballantine.

Nelsen, J., & Glenn, H. S. (1991). *Time out*. Fair Oaks, CA: Sunrise Press.

Neumann, E. (1971). *Art and the creative unconscious: Four essays*. Princeton, NJ: Princeton University Press.

Nylund, D., & Corsiglia, V. (1997). From deficits to special abilities: Working narratively with children labeled ADHD. In M. F. Hoyt (Ed.), *Constructive therapies* (pp. 163–183). New York: Guilford Press.

Oaklander, V. (1978). *Windows to our children*. Moab, UT: Real People Press.

Olds, A. R. (1979). Designing developmentally optimal classrooms for children with special needs. In S. J. Meisels (Ed.), *Special education and development* (pp. 91–138). Baltimore: University Park Press.

Omizo, M. M. (1981, April). Relaxation training and biofeedback with hyperactive elementary school children. *Elementary School Guidance and Counseling, 15*(4), 329–333.

O'Neil, J. (1994, January). Looking at art through new eyes. *Curriculum Update*, pp. 1, 8.

Orlick, T. (1982). *Second cooperative sports and games book*. New York: Pantheon.

Osguthorpe, R. T. (1985, September). Trading places: Why disabled students should tutor non-disabled students. *The Exceptional Parent, 15*(5), 41–48.

Palladino, J. (1997). *The Edison trait: Saving the spirit of your nonconforming child*. New York: Times Books.

Panksepp, J. (1996, Fall). Sensory integration, rough-and-tumble play and ADHD. *Lost and Found: Perspectives on Brain, Emotions, and Culture, 2*(3), 1–3.

Parker, H. C. (1992). *The ADD hyperactivity handbook for schools*. Plantation, FL: Impact Publications.

Patterson, N. H. (1997). *Every body can learn: Engaging the bodily-kinesthetic intelligence in the everyday classroom*. Tucson, AZ: Zephyr Press.

Pelham, W. E., Murphy, D. A., Vannatta, K., Milich, R., Licht, B. G., Gnagy, E. M., Greenslade, K. E., Greiner, A. R., & Vodde-Hamilton, M. (1992). Methylphenidate and attributions in boys with attention-deficit hyperactivity disorder. *Journal of Consulting and Clinical Psychology, 60*(2), 282–292.

Pennington, B. F., Groisser, D., & Welsh, M. C. (1993). Contrasting cognitive deficits in attention deficit hyperactivity disorder versus reading disability. *Developmental Psychology, 29*(3), 511–523.

Perry, B. D., & Pollard, R. (1998). Homeostasis, stress, trauma, and adaptation: A neurodevelopmental view of childhood trauma. *Child & Adolescent Psychiatric Clinics of North America, 7*(1), 33–51.

Phelan, T. W. (1996). *1-2-3-magic*. Child Management.

Porrino, B., Rapoport, J. L., Behar, D., Sceery, W., Ismond, D. R., & Bunney, W. E., Jr. (1983). A naturalistic assessment of the motor activity of hyperactive boys. *Archives of General Psychiatry, 40*, 681–687.

Portner, J. (1993, November 3). 46 states mandate P.E., but only four found to require classes in all grades. *Education Week*, p. 10.

Powell, S., & Nelsen, B. (1997). Effects of choosing academic assignments on a student with attention deficit hyperactivity disorder. *Journal of Applied Behavior Analysis, 30*(1), 181–183.

Putnam, S., & Copans, S. A. (1998, Winter). Exercise: An alternative approach to the treatment of AD/HD. *Reaching Today's Youth, 2,* 66–68.

Rapoport, J. (1995, Winter). Q&A: An interview with Dr. Judith Rapoport, Chief of the Child Psychiatry Branch of the National Institute of Mental Health. *Attention!* Available on the Internet: http://www.chadd.org/attention/rapoport.htm

Ratey, J. J., & Johnson, C. (1998). *Shadow syndromes: The mild forms of major mental disorders that sabotage us.* New York: Bantam/Doubleday/Dell.

Reid, B. D., & McGuire, M. D. (1995). *Square pegs in round holes—these kids don't fit: High ability students with behavioral problems.* Storrs: National Research Center on the Gifted and Talented, University of Connecticut.

Reid, R., & Magg, J. W. (1994). How many fidgets in a pretty much: A critique of behavior rating scales for identifying students with ADHD. *Journal of School Psychology, 32*(3), 339–354.

Reid, R., & Maag, J. W. (1997). Attention deficit hyperactivity disorder: Over here and over there. *Educational and Child Psychology, 14*(1), 10–20.

Reid, R., Maag, J. W., & Vasa, S. F. (1993). Attention deficit hyperactivity disorder as a disability category: A critique. *Exceptional Children, 60*(3): 198–214.

Reif, S. F. (1993). *How to reach and teach ADD/ADHD children.* West Nyack, NY: The Center for Applied Research in Education.

Resnick, R. J., & McEvoy, K. (Eds.). (1994). Attention-deficit/hyperactivity disorder: Abstracts of the psychological and behavioral literature, 1971–1994. *Bibliographies in Psychology, No. 14.* Washington, DC: American Psychological Association.

Richter, N. C. (1984). The efficacy of relaxation training with children. *Journal of Abnormal Child Psychology, 12*(2), 319–344.

Robin, A. (1990). Training families with ADHD adolescents. In R. Barkley (Ed.), *Attention deficit hyperactivity disorder: A handbook for diagnosis and treatment* (pp. 413–457). New York: Guilford Press.

Robinson, H. (1998, November). Are we raising boys wrong? *Ladies Home Journal,* 96–100.

Rose, C. (1989). *Accelerative learning.* New York: Dell.

Rose, F. (1987, November 8). Pied piper of the computer. *The New York Times Magazine,* pp. 56–62, 140–141.

Rosenthal, R. (1978). Interpersonal expectancy effects: The first 345 studies. *The Behavioral and Brain Sciences, 3,* 377–415.

Rosenthal, R., & Jacobson, L. (1968). *Pygmalion in the classroom.* New York: Holt, Rinehart & Winston.

Ross, D., & Ross, S. (1982). *Hyperactivity: Current issues, research, and theory.* New York: Wiley.

Safer, D. J., & Krager, J. M. (1992). Effect of a media blitz and a threatened lawsuit on stimulant treatment. *Journal of the American Medical Association, 268*(8), 1004–1007.

Samples, B. (1976). *The metaphoric mind.* Reading, MA: Addison-Wesley.

Satir, V. (1983). *Conjoint family therapy* (3rd ed.). Palo Alto, CA: Science and Behavior Books.

Schneidler, T. D. (1973, August). *Application of psychosynthesis techniques to child psychotherapy*. Paper presented at the International Conference on Psychosynthesis, Val Morin, QC.

Schrag, P., & Divoky, D. (1975). *The myth of the hyperactive child: And other means of child control*. New York: Pantheon.

Schuster, D. H., & Gritton, C. E. (1986). *Suggestive accelerative learning techniques*. New York: Gordon & Breach

Schwartz, J. (1992). *Another door to learning*. New York: Crossroad.

Schwartz, J. M., Stoeseel, P. W., Baxter, L. R., Martin, K. M., & Phelps, M. E. (1996, February). Systematic changes in cerebral glucose metabolic rate after successful behavior modification treatment of obsessive-compulsive disorder. *Archives of General Psychiatry, 53*, 109–113.

Scott, T. J. (1969). The use of music to reduce hyperactivity in children. *American Journal of Orthopsychiatry, 40*(4), 677–680.

Scrip, L. (1990). *Transforming teaching through arts PROPEL portfolios: A case study of assessing individual student work in the high school ensemble*. Cambridge, MA: Harvard Project Zero.

Seefeldt, V., & Vogel, P. (1990, November). What can we do about physical education? *Principal, 70*, 12–14.

Shaw, G. A., & Brown, G. (1991). Laterality, implicit memory, and attention disorder. *Educational Studies, 17*(1), 25–23.

Sigmon, S. B. (1987). *Radical analysis of special education: Focus on historical development and learning disabilities*. New York: Falmer Press.

Sleator, E. K., & Ullmann, R. L. (1981, January). Can the physician diagnose hyperactivity in the office? *Pediatrics, 67*(1), 13–17.

Sleator, E. K., Ullmann, R. K., & Neumann, A. (1982). How do hyperactive children feel about taking stimulants and will they tell the doctor? *Clinical Pediatrics, 21*(8), 474–479.

Smallwood, D. (1997). *Attention disorders in children: A compilation of resources for school psychologists*. Washington, DC: National Association of School Psychologists.

Smitheman-Brown, V., & Church, R. P. (1996). Mandala drawing: Facilitating creative growth in children with A.D.D. or A.D.H.D. *Art Therapy: Journal of the American Art Therapy Association, 13*(4), 252–260.

Spencer, T., Biederman, J., Wilens, T., Guite, J.(1995, July). ADHD and thyroid abnormalities: A research note. *Journal of Child Psychology & Psychiatry & Allied Disciplines, 36*(5), 879–885.

Spolin, V. (1986). *Theater games for the classroom*. Evanston, IL: Northwestern University Press.

Squires, S. (1990, November 15). Brain function yields physical clue that could help pinpoint hyperactivity. *The Washington Post*, p. A08.

Steiner, R. (1974). *The kingdom of childhood*. London: Rudolf Steiner Press.

Stewart, M. (1993). *Yoga for children*. New York: Fireside.

Still, G. W. (1902, April 12). Some abnormal psychical conditions in children. *The Lancet, 4103*, 1008–1012.

Sudderth, D. B., & Kandel, J. (1997). *Adult ADD: The complete handbook.* Rocklin, CA: Prima Publishing.

Sunshine, J. L., Lewin, J. S., Wu, D. H., Miller, D. A., Findlin, R. L., Manos, M. J., & Schwartz, M. A. (1997). Functional MR to localize sustained visual attention activation in patients with attention deficit hyperactivity disorder: A pilot study. *American Journal of Neuroradiology, 18*(4), 633–637.

Sutherland, J., & Algozzine, B. (1979). The learning disabled label as a biasing factor in the visual motor performance of normal children. *Journal of Learning Disabilities, 12*(1), 8–14.

Sutton-Smith, B. (1998). *The ambiguity of play.* Cambridge, MA: Harvard University Press.

Swanson, J. M., McBurnett, K., Wigal, T., Pfiffner, L. J., Lerner, M. A., Williams, L., Christian, D. L., Tamm, L., Willcutt, E., Crowley, K., Clevenger, W., Khouzam, N., Woo, C., Crinell, F. M., & Fisher, T. D. (1993). Effect of stimulant medication on children with attention deficit disorder: A review of reviews. *Exceptional Children, 60*(2), 154–162.

Sykes, D. H., Douglas, V. I., & Morgenstern, G. (1973). Sustained attention in hyperactive children. *Journal of Child Psychology & Psychiatry & Allied Disciplines, 14,* 213–220.

Sylwester, R. (1995). *A celebration of neurons.* Alexandria, VA: Association for Supervision and Curriculum Development.

Sylwester, R., & Cho, J. -Y. (1992, December–1993, January). What brain research says about paying attention. *Educational Leadership, 50,* 71–75.

Taylor, D. (1991). *Learning denied.* Portsmouth, NH: Heinemann.

Taylor, E., & Sandberg, S. (1984). Hyperactive behavior in English schoolchildren: A questionnaire survey. *Journal of Abnormal Child Psychology, 12*(1), 143–155.

Thomas, A., Chess, S., Sillen, J., & Menzez, O. (1974). Cross-cultural study of behavior in children with special vulnerabilities to stress. In D. Ricks, A. Thomas, & M. Roff (Eds.), *Life history research in psychopathology: Vol. 3.* Minneapolis: University of Minnesota Press.

Turecki, S. (1989). *The difficult child.* New York: Bantam.

Turecki, S. (1995). *Normal children have problems, too: How parents can understand and help.* New York: Bantam/Doubleday/Dell.

Tyson, K. (1991). The understanding and treatment of childhood hyperactivity: Old problems and new approaches. *Smith College Studies in Social Work, 61*(1), 133–166.

Vaidya, C. J., Austin, G., Kirkorian, G., Ridlehuber, H. W., Desmond, J. E., Glover, G. H., & Gabrieli, J. D. E. (1998). Selective effects of methylphenidate in attention deficit hyperactivity disorder: A functional magnetic resonance study. *Proceedings of the National Academy of Science, 95*(24), 14494–14499.

Viadero, D. (1991, October 2). E. D. clarifies policy on attention-deficit disorder. *Education Week,* p. 29.

Virgilio, S. J., & Berenson, G. S. (1988). Super kids—superfit: A comprehensive fitness intervention model for elementary schools. *Journal of Physical Education, Recreation, and Dance, 59*(8), 19–25.

Volkow, N. D., Ding, Y. -S., Fowler, J. S., Wang, G. -J., Logan, J., Gatley, J. S., Dewey, S.,

Ashby, C., Liebermann, J., Hitzemann, R., & Wolf, A. P.(1995). Is methylphenidate like cocaine? *Archives of General Psychiatry, 52*, 456–463.

Vygotsky, L. S. (1986). *Thought and language*. Cambridge, MA: MIT Press.

Wallace, R. (1992). *Rappin' and rhyming: Raps, songs, cheers, and smartrope jingles for active learning*. Tucson, AZ: Zephyr.

Wallis, C. (1994, July 18). Life in overdrive. *Time, 144*(3), 43–50.

Walther, M., & Beare, P. (1991). The effect of videotape feedback on the on-task behavior of a student with emotional/behavioral disorders. *Education and Treatment of Children, 14*(1), 53–60.

Weinstein, C. S. (1979). The physical environment of the school: A review of the research. *Review of Educational Research, 49*(4), 585.

Weiss, L. (1997). *ADD and creativity*. Dallas, TX: Taylor Publishing.

Whalen, C. K., & Henker, B. (Eds.). (1980). *Hyperactive children: The social ecology of identification and treatment*. New York: Academic Press.

Whalen, C. K., & Henker, B. (1991). Therapies for hyperactive children: Comparisons, combinations, and compromises. *Journal of Consulting and Clinical Psychology, 59*(1), 126–137.

Whalen, C. K., Henker, B., Hinshaw, S. P., Heller, T., & Huber-Dressler, A. (1991). Messages of medication: Effects of actual versus informed medication status on hyperactive boys' expectancies and self-evaluations. *Journal of Consulting and Clinical Psychology, 59*(4), 602–606.

Williams, M. (1996). *Cool cats, calm kids: Relaxation and stress management for young people*. San Luis Obispo, CA: Impact.

Woltersdorf, M. A. (1992). Videotape self-modeling in the treatment of attention-deficit hyperactivity disorder. *Child and Family Behavior Therapy, 14*(2), 53–73.

Yelich, G., & Salamone, F. J. (1994). Constructivist interpretation of attention-deficit hyperactivity disorder. *Journal of Constructivist Psychology, 7*(3), 191–212.

Zagar, R., & Bowers, N. D. (1983, July). The effect of time of day on problem solving and classroom behavior. *Psychology in the Schools, 20*, 337–345.

Zametkin, A. J., Nordahl, T. E., Gross, M., King, A. C., Semple, W. E., Rumsey, J., Hamburger, S., & Cohen, R. M. (1990, November 15). Cerebral glucose metabolism in adults with hyperactivity of childhood onset. *New England Journal of Medicine, 323*(20), 1413–1416.

Zametkin, A. J., Liebenauer, L. L., Fitzgerald, G. A., King, A. C., Minkunas, D. V., Herscovitch, P., Yamada, E. M., & Cohen, R. M. (1993, May). Brain metabolism in teenagers with attention-deficit hyperactivity disorder. *Archives of General Psychiatry, 50*, 333–340.

Zentall, S. (1975). Optimal stimulation as a theoretical basis of hyperactivity. *American Journal of Orthopsychiatry, 45*(4), 549–563.

Zentall, S. (1980). Behavioral comparisons of hyperactive and normally active children in natural settings. *Journal of Abnormal Child Psychology, 8*(1), 93–109.

Zentall, S. (1988). Production deficiencies in elicited language but not in the spontaneous verbalizations of hyperactive children. *Journal of Abnormal Child Psychology, 16*(6), 657–673.

Zentall, S. (1993a). Research on the educational implications of attention deficit hyperactivity disorder. *Exceptional Children, 60*(2), 143–153.

Zentall, S. (1993b). Outcomes of ADD: Academic and social performance and their related school and home treatments. *CH.A.D.D. Fourth Annual Conference, Chicago, October 15–17, 1992* (Transcripts of Presentations). Plantation, FL: CH.A.D.D.

Zentall, S., & Kruczek, T. (1988). The attraction of color for active attention-problem children. *Exceptional Children, 54*(4), 357–362.

Zentall, S., & Zentall, T. R. (1976) Activity and task performance of hyperactive children as a function of environmental stimulation. *Journal of Consulting and Clinical Psychology, 44*(5), 693–697.

Zentall, S., & Zentall, T. R. (1983). Optimal stimulation: A model of disordered activity and performance in normal and deviant children. *Psychological Bulletin, 94*(3), 446–471.

Zoldan, D. (1997, July 23). Ritalin teens can forget about the military. (Scripps Howard News Service).

INDEX

accelerative learning, 63–64
ACLD. *See* Association for Children with
  Learning Disabilities
ADD/ADHD
    assessment of, 2
    assumptions about, 2
    becoming household term, 1
    as biological disorder, 2, 3–8, 16–17
    biological studies about, 3–8
    cross-cultural studies, 32–33
    definition, instability of, 10–11,
      19, 24
    developmental perspectives on,
      38–42
    diagnosis, assumptions about, 2,
      11–14
    discounting of psychotherapeutic
      approaches to, 45
    educational approaches to. *See*
      affective, behavioral, biological,
      cognitive, ecological, education-
      al, and physical strategies
    environmental factors, 4
    first observations of, 22–23
    genetic and environmental origins
      of, 7–8
    government benefits available for,
      26
    as historical movement, 23–24, 28
    history of, 22–23
    holistic approach to, 18–19, 21, 48,
      49–57, 73
    incidence, assumptions about, 2,
      10–11

    and learning styles, 36
    longevity, assumptions about, 2,
      17–19, 38–39
    nonmedical approaches, 15, 16
    overdiagnosis of, 2
    personal emotions of children diag-
      nosed with, 80–81
    presence with other disorders,
      assumptions about, 2, 19–21
    reasons for growth of, 24–28
    scenarios, 27–28
    symptoms
        assumptions about, 2, 8–9
        similar to creative traits,
          33–35
        similar to difficult child
          traits, 47
        as untapped creative poten-
          tial, 83
    treatment, assumptions about, 2,
      14–17.
    without hyperactivity, 69
ADD/ADHD adult, 17
ADD/ADHD paradigm, vi–vii, 1, 2,
  49–50
    adjustments in to accommodate
      new findings, 20–21, 34
    alternatives to, 22
    assumptions of, 2–21
    childlike traits, 41–42
    cognitive perspective, 33–35, 53
    continued growth of, 103
    criticism of, 9, 22
    dangers of, 44–45

developmental perspective, 38–42,
    53–55
educational perspective, 35–38
gender differences perspective,
    42–43
historical perspective, 22–28
holistic approach, 48–55
insensitivity to developmental vari-
    ations, 40
limited understanding of human
    psyche, 44–45
movement from biological to
    developmental, 18
as negative rather than positive,
    53–55
psychoaffective perspective, 43–48
Ritalin and, 15
sociocultural perspective, 28–33
structure of assumptions about, 2–3
traditional, 49–50
ADHD (attention-deficit-hyperactivity
    disorder). See ADD/ADHD
Adler, Alfred, 45
affective strategies, 80–87
    expressive arts, 82–83
    positive image-holding, 83–85
    positive role models, 85–87
aggressiveness, related to overcrowded
    conditions, 91
alpha waves, 72
alternative research studies, 57
American Pediatric Association, 79
"American problem," 40–41
American Psychiatric Association, 10, 24
Ames, Louise Bates, 41
anxiety, 43–44
anxiety disorders, 19
appropriate movement, allowing, 74–76
Armstrong, Louis, 86
arts-oriented activities, 82
assessment, authentic, 54, 59, 60
Association for Children with Learning
    Disabilities, 25
associative minds, 70
attention, studies of, 5, 25

attention-deficit disorder. See also
    ADD/ADHD
    as cognitive construct, 67
    first use of term, 23
    as reflection of societal breakdown,
        29
    and traditional values, 31
attention-deficit-hyperactivity disorder.
    See ADD/ADHD

Barkley, Russell, 10, 36
Beethoven, 86
behavioral spectrum, 47–48
behavioral strategies, 96–101
    behavioral feedback, 100–101
    collaborative discipline, 97–98
    time out, 98–100
behaviorism, 24
behavior modification, 62, 96–97
behavior rating scales, 12–13
Benson, Herbert, 71
Bernhardt, Sarah, 86
beta waves, 72
biofeedback, 68, 71–73
biological paradigm
    insufficiency of, 48–49
    as part of holistic approach,
        51–52
    predominance of, 35–36
    replacement of with focus on
        whole child, 50–51
biological perspective, 54
biological strategies, 101–102
bioreductionism, 8
bodily-kinesthetic learners, 37, 73
brain activity, continuous performance
    tasks, 13–14
brain metabolism, 3–4
brain structure, 4–5
breathing exercise, 76, 77
buddy programs, 89

Cartwright, Samuel, 31–32
central-task attention, 62–63
cerebral glucose metabolism, 3

CH.A.D.D. (Children and Adults with Attention Deficit Disorders), 26, 58
change, penchant for, 42–43
Chess, Stella, 46
"choice time," 64
chronopsychology, 93
Churchill, Winston, 42, 85
circadian rhythms, 93
class meetings, 88, 89
classroom management. See behavioral and interpersonal strategies; learning environments
classroom setting, adjustment to, 58
cocaine, similarity of Ritalin to, 15
cognitive approaches, mixed results of, 68
cognitive paradigm, 52
cognitive perspective, 33–35, 53, 54
cognitive psychology, 24–25
cognitive strategies, 67–73
    biofeedback, 71–73
    focusing techniques, 71
    self-talk, 68–69
    visualization, 69–70
collaborative discipline, 97–98
comorbid factors, 19, 20, 23, 43–44, 49
computer technology, 66–67
confounding variables, 19
continuous performance tasks, 12, 13–14
cooperative learning, 37
Copernicus, Nicolaus, v, 103
CPT. See continuous performance tasks
creative traits, similarity to ADD/ADHD symptoms, 33–35
cross-age tutoring, 88–89
cultural differences, 54
curriculum
    culturally sensitive, 54
    developmentally appropriate, 54
    and expressive arts, 83
    gifted and talented, 54
    and holistic approaches, 73
    and individualized learning, 38
    and multiple intelligences, 60
    and physical movement, 75–76
    and visualization and imagination, 70

deficit paradigm, 87
depression, 44, 54
developmental concerns, 49
developmentally inappropriate practices, 40–41
developmental paradigm, 18–19, 52
developmental perspective, 38–42, 53–55
developmental stages, 40–41
Diagnostic and Statistical Manual of Mental Disorders, 4th edition (DSM-IV), 10, 11, 18, 24
difficult child, 46–47
distractibility, 2, 8–9, 19, 20, 39, 41
    effect of Ritalin on, 15
    gender differences perspective, 43
    as misdirected energy, 82
    nonlinear thinking categorized as, 66
    psychoaffective perspective, 43
    unconscious ignored in study of, 45
dopamine D4 receptor gene, 6–7
double-blind placebo controlled studies, 56–57
drapetomania, 31–32
Driven to Distraction (Hallowell & Ratey), 27
DSM-IV. See Diagnostic and Statistical Manual of Mental Disorders, 4th edition

easy child, 46
ecological strategies, 90–96. See also learning environments
    food, 95–96
    sound, 94–95
    space, 91–93
    time, 93–94
educational guidelines, 58
educational innovations, 59
educational perspective, 35–38, 52, 54
educational strategies, 57–67
    educational technology, 59, 65–67
    incidental learning, 59, 61–64
    multiple intelligences, 59–61
Elkind, David, 40, 43
emotional disturbance, 81

emotional trauma, 44, 54
environment, role of, 4, 7
Erikson, Erik, 45
Escalante, Jaime, 63
experts on key perspectives of ADD/ADHD, 54
expressive arts, 81, 82–83
external locus of control, 55

family systems theory and approaches, 45–46, 49
family therapy, 54
feedback. See behavioral strategies
focusing techniques, 71
food, 95–96, 102
Forbes magazine, 43
Freud, Sigmund, 45

Galilei, Galileo, v
Gardner, Howard, 59
gender differences perspective, 42–43
genetic studies, 5–8
Giedd, J. N., 4–5
Glasser, William, 89
global attention, 33–34
"go, look, and listen" strategy, 74
Goodwin, Brian, 8
Grinspoon, Lester, 29
guided imagery, 70

hands-on learning, 74, 77–79
haptic learners, 77–78
Harvard Educational Review (Grinspoon & Singer), 29
heritability, 7
"high movers," 74
high-stimulation environment, 37, 92. See *also* learning environments
historical perspective, 22–28
Hobbs, Nicholas, 31
holistic approach, 18–19, 21, 48, 49–55, 56, 57, 73
holistic schematic, 51–55
Hubbard, Ruth, 6
hyperactive, 23
hyperactive heroes, 86

hyperactivity, 2, 8–9, 13, 19, 20, 39, 41, 45, 65
    controlled with diet, 96
    effect of Ritalin on, 15
    gender differences perspective, 43
    as misdirected energy, 82
    psychoaffective perspective, 43
hyper-focus, 20
hyperkinesis, 29
hyperkinetic, 23
hypertext, 65
hypoactivity, 13

Illich, Ivan, 31
imagery, 76
imagination, 70
immaturity. See neoteny
impulsivity, 2, 8–9, 19, 39, 41
    effect of Ritalin on, 15
    gender differences perspective, 43
    as misdirected energy, 82
    psychoaffective perspective, 43
    unconscious ignored in study of, 45
incidental attention, 33, 62–63
incidental learning, 59, 61–64
inner speech, 68
interdisciplinary approach, 48–49
internalizing of ADD/ADHD behavior, 39–40
Internet, 65, 67
interpersonal strategies, 87–90
    class meetings, 89
    cross-age tutoring, 88–89
    peer tutoring, 88–89
    positive social moments, 89–90
interventions, examples of, 54
introspection, 71
isometrics, 76

Jung, Carl, 45

Kepler, Johannes, 20–21
kinesthetic imagery, 77
knowledge units, 65
Kuhn, Thomas S., v

labeling, stigma of, 55
labels, use of, 32, 35, 37
learned helplessness, 55
learning, 35–36, 49
learning disabilities, 6, 19, 25
learning environments, 36–38, 58–59
learning styles, 36, 54, 84
legislative support, 25–26
Lozanov, Georgi, 63

magnetic resonance imaging (MRI), 3.
    See also MRI studies
male liberation movement, 43
manipulatives, math, 78
marketplace for ADD/ADHD products,
    26–27, 56
Matching Familiar Figures Test, 14
math bathtub, 75
Meaney, Michael, 7
media attention, 27-28
medical exams, 12, 54
medical-model diagnosis, 48–50. See also
    biological paradigm
meditation, 71
methyphenidate hydrochloride. See
    Ritalin
MFFT. See Matching Familiar Figures Test
minimal brain damage, 23
Molecular Biology, 6
mood disorders, 19
movement, 73, 74–76
MRI studies, 4–5, 13–14
multiple-disorder approach, 19
multiple intelligences, 37–38, 59–61, 84
music, effect of, 94–95
myelinization, 40

negative labeling, 83
neoteny, 41–42, 55
neurobiological differences, 44, 52, 54
New Orleans Medical and Surgical Journal,
    31
Newsweek magazine, 27
nondirected learning, 61–62
nonlinear mind, 65–66

nonmedical approaches, 15, 16
novelty-seeking behavior, 6–7

off-task behavior, 64
Olds, Anita, 91
"1–2–3–Magic!" 99
"Oprah," 27

Panksepp, Jaak, 80
paradigm, v–vii, 20–21. See also
    ADD/ADHD paradigm
parent advocacy groups, 25–26, 29
peer tutoring, 88–89
personal emotions, 80–81
PET scan studies, 3–4
physical education program, 74, 79–80
physicality, 73
physical strategies, 73–80
    appropriate movement, allowing,
        74–76
    hands-on learning, 77–79
    movement, 73
    physical education, 79–80
    physical relaxation skills, 76–77
Piaget, Jean, 40, 41
play, importance of, 64
Pope John XXIII, 86
positive image-holding, 81, 83–85
positive role models, 81, 85–87
positive social moments, 89–90
positron emission tomography. See PET
    scan studies
private speech, 64, 69
progressive relaxation, 76–77
psychoaffective perspective, 43–48, 54
psychoanalysis, 25
psychobiology, 25
psychodynamic approaches, 44, 45–48
psychological testing, 12, 14
psychopharmaceutical treatment, 25. See
    also Ritalin
psychotherapy, 54
Ptolemy, 20, 103
Public Law 94-142, the Education for All
    Handicapped Children Act, 25–26

questions and answers, 54

radiant child, 103
reflection, 71
relaxation, 76–77
responsibility, sense of, 15
reverie, 71
Ritalin, 14–17, 48, 58–59, 79, 101
    backlash response to, 16
    as behavioral Band Aid, 44
    effectiveness of, 14–15
    drawbacks of, 15–16
    as one treatment among many, 17
rites of passage, 71
roaming meditation, 71
rough-and-tumble play, 80

scapegoating, 46
Schwartz, Jeffrey M., 4
self-esteem, 55
self-talk, 68–69, 70
short-attention-span culture, 30, 65
Singer, Susan B., 29
Skinnerian principles, 96–97
slow-to-warm child, 46
social difficulties, 87
social skills programs, 87
sociocultural perspective, 28–33, 54
sound, 94–95
space, 91–93
Stand and Deliver, 63
Still, George, 22
stimulation, 58–59
"stop, look, and listen" strategy criticized, 73
strategies and techniques for helping children learn. See affective, behavioral, biological, cognitive, ecological, educational, and physical strategies
stress, 7
The Structure of Scientific Revolutions (Kuhn), v
students. See ADD/ADHD; holistic approach
substance-abuse problems, 15–16

subtyping, 20, 23, 34
suggestopedia, 63
super-learning, 63–64
symptoms. See ADD/ADHD

tai-chi, 71
teachers. See also affective, behavioral, biological, cognitive, ecological, educational, and physical strategies
    and behavior management, 96–101
    and behavior rating scales, 12–13
    and children's movement in the classroom, 74–76
    and circadian rhythms, 93–94
    and classroom space, 91–93
    as curriculum developers, 60
    and "educational questions," 38
    as experts, among other professionals, 54
    and hands-on activities, 78
    holding a positive image of the child with ADD/ADHD, 83–85
    and incidental learning, 61–64
    and perceived authority of, 29
    preschool, 41
    and Ritalin's effects, 14–17, 44
    role in promoting social skills, 87
    role in understanding child's learning styles, 35–38
    and "self-talk," 68–69
team-based approach, 48–49
technology, educational, 59, 65–67
television, 30
temperaments, 84
temperament studies, 46–48
testing, and subjective judgments, 12–13
theta waves, 72
Thomas, Alexander, 46
thyroid disorder, 6
time, 93–94
Time magazine, 27
time out, 98-100
traditional ADD/ADHD paradigm, 49–50
traditional model of education, 73

treatments, 56
Turecki, Stanley, 47

visionary quests, 71
visualization, 68, 69–70, 77, 85

Wechsler Intelligence Scale for Children,
   14

whole-child focus, 50–51
Wisconsin Card Sort Test, 14

yoga, 71, 76, 80

Zametkin, A. J., 3–4, 6
Zentall, Sydney, 58–59

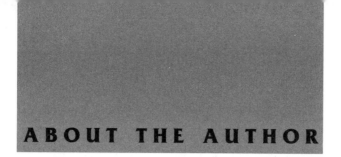

ABOUT THE AUTHOR

Thomas Armstrong is an educator and psychologist with more than 26 years of teaching experience, from the primary through the doctoral level. He is the author of nine books, including *The Myth of the A.D.D. Child: 50 Ways to Improve Your Child's Behavior and Attention Span without Drugs, Labels, or Coercion* (New York: Plume, 1997) and two ASCD books, *Multiple Intelligences in the Classroom* and *Awakening Genius in the Classroom*. He can be reached by mail at P.O. Box 548, Cloverdale, CA 95425; by phone at 707-894-4646; by fax at 707-894-4474; by e-mail at thomas@thomasarmstrong.com; or by visiting his Web site (http://www.thomasarmstrong.com).

Related ASCD Resources: Inclusive Classroom Practices

Audiotapes

Curriculum Development: A Framework for All Students, 1999 ASCD Annual
   Conference

Different Needs, Different Answers: An Urban System's Response for the Future,
   1999 ASCD Annual Conference

CD-ROMs

The Curriculum Handbook CD-ROM

Educational Leadership CD-ROM

Exploring Our Multiple Intelligences

Online Courses

Multiple Intelligences Professional Development Online (available on the Internet:
   http://www.ascd.org)

Print Products

ASCD Topic Pack—*Multiple Intelligences*

Awakening Genius in the Classroom by Thomas Armstrong

Creating an Inclusive School by Richard A. Villa and Jacqueline S. Thousand

Multiple Intelligences and Student Achievement: Success Stories from Six Schools by
   Linda Campbell and Bruce Campbell

Multiple Intelligences in the Classroom by Thomas Armstrong

Students with Special Needs, *Educational Leadership*, Vol. 53, No.5, February
   1996

Videotapes

Beyond the ADD Myth: Classroom Strategies and Techniques, featuring Thomas
   Armstrong

Inclusion, developed in cooperation with the Council for Exceptional Children

The Multiple Intelligences Series, featuring Howard Gardner

What's New in School—A Parent's Guide to Inclusion

For additional resources, visit us on the World Wide Web (http://www.ascd.org),
send an e-mail message to member@ascd.org, call the ASCD Service Center (1-
800-933-ASCD or 703-578-9600, then press 2), send a fax to 703-575-5400, or
write to Information Services, ASCD, 1703 N. Beauregard St., Alexandria, VA
22311-1714 USA.